THE VATICAN

The Basilica of ST. PETER - The Sistine Chapel - The Museums - The Gardens

EDITRICE MA.PI.R.
del Cav. Uff. Mario PIETRANGELI
Via delle Fornaci 147/155
00165 Roma - Tel. 6377089-6375259

INDEX

Page

This book is intended to be a modest but useful contribution to the knowledge and wider awareness of the artistic treasures of the Vatican City. Through the various tours, the choice of works of art, the very careful research into historical events, the analysis of the artistic content, the popular presentation and the generous provision of photographs, we have sought to make this publication a really valuable aid to visiting what must be considered to be one of the greatest treasures of our whole civilisation.

The Author

Some reproductions were granted by the photographic Archives of the Vatican Museums and by the "Reverenda Fabbrica" of St. Peter in Vatican.

Translation by
BRIAN WILLIAMS

(St. Peter's Square)

Aerial view of St Peter's Square and the Vatican City ▶

THE VATICAN CITY

The Vatican State is one of the smallest in the world, with an area of less than 440,000 square metres. It is an independent state, under the sovereignty of the Pope, as established by the Lateran Pacts — an agreement between Italy and the Holy See signed on 11th February 1929.

Despite its limitations of size, the Vatican City owns a treasury of masterpieces of art and architecture which is unique in the world: in its territory are included the Piazza of Saint Peter and the Basilica itself, the Vatican Palaces, where many of the Museums are housed, a number of Churches, the splendid gardens, the Audience Chamber by Pier Luigi Nervi, a railway station and a helicopter port, and a radio transmitting station.

The Vatican city-state, as well as issuing its own stamps, has a mint where it coins its own money; it has its services of law and order and its police system, carried on by the Agenti di Vigilanza, set up in 1816, and the Swiss Guard, a body which has been in existence since 1506; the Guards still wear the multi-coloured uniforms which are said to have been designed for them by Michelangelo himself.

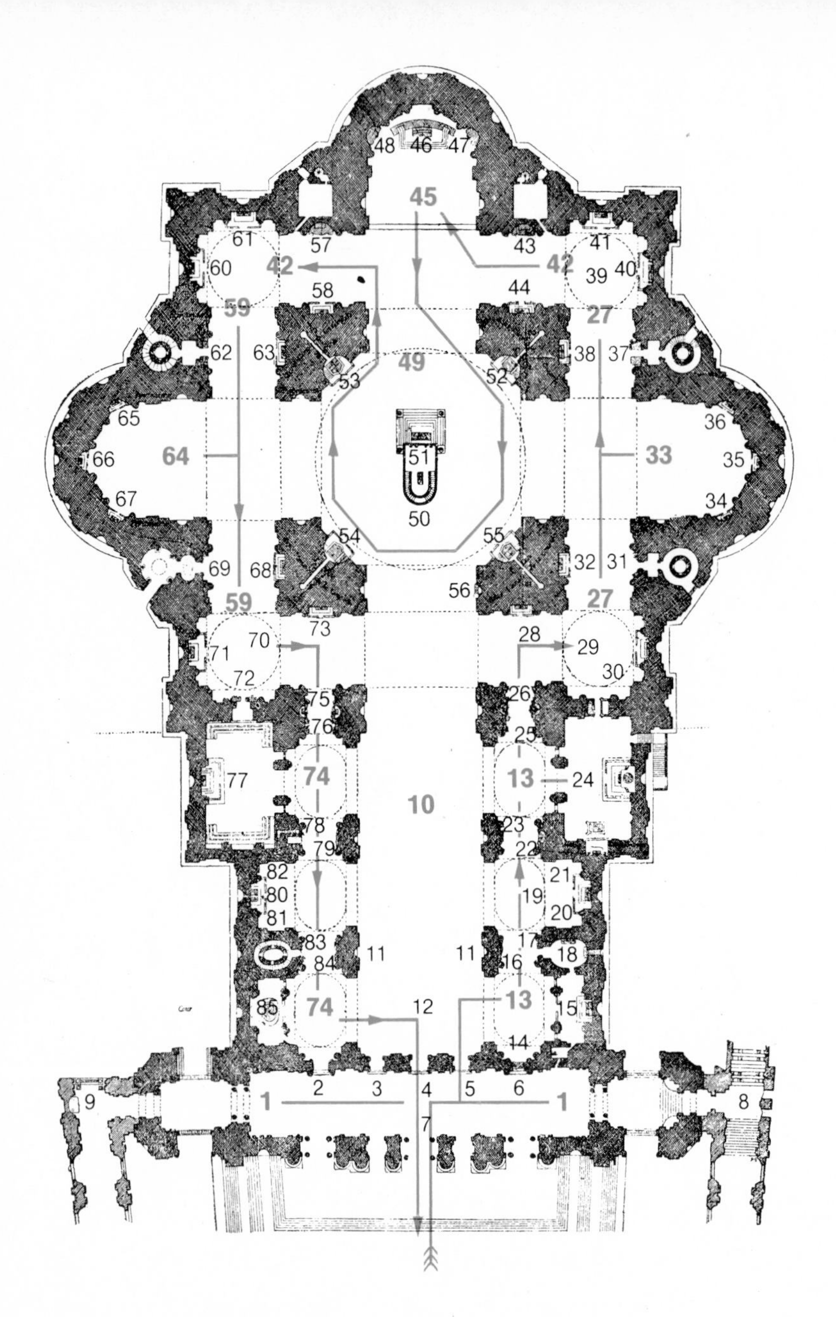

REFERENCES IN THE PLAN

1. **Atrium**
2. Doorway of Manzù
3. Doorway of Minguzzi
4. Doorway of Filarete
5. Doorway of Crocetti
6. The Holy Door (Porta Sancta)
7. Mosaic of the Little Ship
8. Statue of Constantine
9. Statue of Charlemagne

10. **Main nave**
11. Holy Water Stoup
12. Disc of the coronation

13. **Right aisle**
14. Mosaic of St. Peter
15. Chapel of the Pietà
16. Monument to Christine of Sweden
17. Monument to Leo XII
18. Chapel of the Crucifix
19. Chapel of St. Sebastian
20. Monument to Pius XI
21. Monument to Pius XII
22. Monument to Innocent XII
23. Monument to Matilda of Canossa
24. Chapel of the Sacrament
25. Monument to Gregory XIII
26. Monument to Gregory XIV
27. Altar of St. Jerome

28. **Right hand side of the transept**
29. Gregorian Chapel
30. Monument to Gregory XVI
31. Monument to Benedict XIV
32. Altar of St. Basil the Great
33. Right wing of the Transept
34. Altar of St. Wenceslas
35. Altar of Sts. Proculus and Martius
36. Altar of St. Erasmus
37. Monument to Clement XIII
38. Altar of the Little Ship
39. Chapel of St. Michael
40. Altar of St. Michael
41. Altar of St. Petronilla

42. **End and retrochoir of the church**
43. Monument to Clement X
44. Altar of Tabitha
45. Apse
46. Throne of St. Peter
47. Monument to Urban VIII
48. Monument to Paul III
49. Baldacchino
50. Confessio
51. Tomb of St. Peter
52. Pillar of St. Helena
53. Pillar of the Veronica
54. Pillar of St. Andrew
55. Pillar of St. Longinus
56. Statue of St. Peter
57. Monument to Alexander VIII
58. Altar of the Paralytic

59. **Left-hand side of the transept**
60. Chapel of the column
61. Altar of St. Leo the Great
62. Monument to Alexander VII
63. Altar of the Sacred Heart of Jesus
64. Left wing of the Transept
65. Altar of St. Thomas
66. Altar of St. Joseph
67. Altar of the Cross of St. Peter
68. Altar of the Lie
69. Monument to Pius VIII
70. Clementine Chapel
71. Altar of St. Gregory the Great
72. Monument to Pius VII
73. Altar of the Transfiguration

74. **Left-hand aisle**
75. Monument to Leo XI
76. Monument to Innocent XI
77. Choir Chapel
78. Monument to St. Pius X
79. Monument to Innocent VIII
80. Chapel of the Presentation
81. Monument to Benedict XV
82. Monument to John XXIII
83. Monument to M. Clementina Sobiesk
84. Monument to the Stuarts
85. Chapel of the Baptismal Font

Fresco by Cesare Nebbia in the Vatican Library with the old Basilica of St. Peter already nearly dismantled, and the new one under construction

THE HISTORY OF THE BASILICA

The building of the ancient Basilica of Saint Peter's, on the initiative of the Emperor Constantine, met with considerable difficulties right from the start, because of the nature of the place where the original shrine of the martyr stood; the so-called "Red Wall", covered with inscriptions, divided the shrine from the other tombs of a Christian cemetery which stood near the Circus of Caligula and Nero. It was the Emperor's firm intention that the "memorial" to the Martyr should be included in the foundations of the apse of his Basilica. The work of levelling off the ground was begun around 330, using a building technique which caused the shrine to be covered over with slabs of pavonazetto and porphyry marble, walled in with wood, and then covered again in marble on the outside. Four columns stood at the corners of this ancient tomb, supporting a baldacchino made up of a pointed trabeation and an architrave. The shrine was illuminated by a great golden candelabra in the form of a crown, containing perhaps as many as fifty lights, while four large silver candlesticks, finely decorated, were placed within the shrine itself.

After twenty five years of work, the Basilica was revealed in all its magnificence as the result of Constantine's lavish generosity. It was mentioned in the Liber Pontificalis that the Emperor himself, as a penance, had filled twelve buckets with earth during the works, and had carried them himself, proud of undertaking such a task.

Reconstructions and drawings of the ancient Basilica, the most important of which is the one by Tiberio Alfarano, make it clear that in front of it there stood a broad square portico decorated with mosaics; this was possibly built under Pope Simplicius (464 - 483), and it was known as "Paradise". The area within this portico measured 50 metres by 47, at the centre of which stood the spring used for the sacred ablutions beneath four Ionic columns supporting a baldacchino with a bronze grill decorated with figures of peacocks, a symbol of the immortality of the soul. At the centre of the marble basin decorated with griffins (the mythical winged beast which in christian symbolism represented the double nature of Christ - human and divine) the water flowed from an enormous bronze pine-cone of the Roman era, which had also been adopted as a symbol of Christ. It came from the district which still bears the name "Pigna" today, between the Pantheon and Piazza Venezia; later on it was placed in the niche of the Belvedere (Courtyard of the Pine).

The portico, during the course of the centuries, was to be the burial place of Popes, Eastern Emperors and other famous people.

The façade of the Church was a simple structure, and according to Cerrati it was adorned with a mosaic of the Saviour amid the Twelve Apostles. Five doors in the façade corresponded with the five internal naves: the *Porta judicii* (reserved for funerals), the Porta Argentea (so-called because it was covered with silver); the Porta Romana (where the symbols of victory were placed), the Porta Ravenniana (referring to Trastevere which was then known as "civitas Ravennatium") and the Porta Guidonea (where the "guidones", who showed the Basilica to the pilgrims, used to gather. This last door gave access to the oratory constructed under Pope John VII, dedicated to Our Lady; later on the cloth known as the Veronica was placed here.

The interior of the Basilica consisted of a massive hall divided up into five naves of four rows each containing twenty two pillars. The columns of the central nave, a good deal higher than those of the side ones, and three times their width, were crowned by a rectilinear trabeation, above which there were arched windows. The colonnades of the side aisles were linked by smaller arches.

The roof consisted of a double slope with a tympanum for the central nave, and a single sloping roof on either side covering both the lateral aisles.

The basic character of the architectural structure contrasted with the minute detail of the floor - "vermiculatum atque exornatum", as Alfarano describes it (intricately inlaid and ornate).

The central nave, with both its walls decorated by twenty four frescoes of scenes from the Old and New Testaments, ended in a triumphal archway at the point where the altar stood, right at the meeting point with the transverse area or transept.

Following the lines of the nave, but lying beyond the transept, was the apse, entirely decorated with mosaics portraying Saint Peter as Head of the Church; both the apse and the transept were closed off by an iron grill and by twisted columns which Bernini was to use in the seventeenth century for his Loggia over the Reliquary.

From the High Middle Ages onwards, the Basilica of St.Peter's was a place of constant pilgrimage; people from every nation came to pay their respects "ad corpus" - i.e. in the actual place where the remains of the Prince of the Apostles were kept, the Sanctuary of Christendom. When they reached the Basilica, they could see through a hole in the marble slab which covered the tomb of Peter, the gold cross offered by Constantine, said to weigh 150 pounds.

During the course of the centuries, the Basilica was a source of special concern to the Popes, who all sought to leave some mark of their pontificate, either by embellishing the church or by restoring it. Among the most notable were Gregory the Great, who raised the floor level, and Calixtus II who consecrated a new high altar.

The barbarian invasions did not detract at all from the ancient Basilica, even though it was very richly adorned with precious metals - only the Saracens in 846 put it to the sack, and among other things they carried off was the cross of Constantine. Despite this, the Basilica was restored to new splendours, because of the keen interest taken in it not only by the Popes but also by simple christian people. For a thousand years the history of Rome itself was intimately linked with that of the Basilica, where frequent dramatic and violent incidents contrasted with the mystical splendours of religious events.

In 1452, when serious damage was discovered inside the Basilica, Pope Nicholas V charged Bernardo Rossellino with drawing up plans for its restoration. From this moment there began that feverish process of architectural activity which was to lead to the destruction of this ancient Basilica and the beginning of the age-long task of constructing the present one.

Rossellino's plans provided for the use of the whole area of the old Basilica and the construction of a portico which would lead in to the new church - still of five naves width, but now in the shape of a Latin Cross, crowned by a dome and terminating in an apse.

When Nicholas V died in 1455, the idea of a complete restoration was abandoned. His successor Pius II (1458 - 1464) only added a loggia for benedictions, and began work on a restoration of the façade, and in the pontificates of Paul II (1464 - 1471), Sixtus IV (1471 - 84), Innocent VIII (1484 - 92) and Alexander VI (1492 - 1503), all idea of reconstruction was given up.

Within the context of a general revival of urban planning and building, and a constant attempt to assert the power and magnificence of the Papacy, Julius II (1503 - 1513), the outstanding exponent of Renaissance ideas, was deeply committed to the idea of building a new basilica. The obvious choice for designing the new project was Giuliano da Sangallo, but the Pope preferred Donato Bramante - perhaps because he was attracted by the grandiose nature of Bramante's plans, which probably originated in one of Leonardo da Vinci's ideas-.Bramante's plan envisaged a church based on a central axis, in the form of a Greek Cross, with an apse at the end of each of the arms. Between one apse and another, as a kind of linking element, was a square building with an internal dome and an external bell-tower, so that the great tower which would stand at the central meeting-point of the four arms, would be surrouded by four minor ones. The general pattern of the intended exterior is known from a commemorative medal by Caradosso, coined by Julius II.

The conception of this plan provided a synthesis between the classical notion of the great dome which would resemble that of the Pantheon, and of the internal pilasters, and the typically sixteenth-century scheme - the whole would have been charged through with the christian humanist ethos.

On 18th April 1506 work began, but it was interrupted by the death of Bramante in 1514, a year later than that of Julius II himself. Of the work which he had projected only the supporting pillars of the dome, the four great central arches and part of the pendentives of the hemisphere had been finished. Before he died, the artist had entrusted the completion of this work to his compatriot Raphael of Urbino, and the latter then drew up a new plan with the collaboration of Giuliano da Sangallo and Fra' Giocondo da Verona. The new plan showed marked differences from that of Bramante, in that a Latin Cross shape was substituted for the Greek one, so that the plan charged from a square basis to a rectangular one. A great pro-naos with a colonnade was to lead into the Basilica, which would have three naves and three apses, while the great dome at the central point of the crossing was to be retained; This plan was judged to be too costly, but it was also set aside because Raphael's death intervened in 1520.

Antonio da Sangallo the Younger was in charge of the works on the building of St. Peter's between 1534 and 1546, aided by Baldassarre Peruzzi. He sought to find a simpler solution for the difficulties of Raphael's earlier project, and at the same time to consolidate the structures that Bramante had left, by adding apsidal bays and restoring the towers. This plan would have provided among other things for the Dome to be supported on two concentric drums, unequal in size, with a lantern surrounded with small columns to crown it.

After the death of Sangallo, Michelangelo entered the scene, when he was nominated Architect for life of the Vatican by Pope Paul III. Michelangelo returned to Bramante 's original project of the central system with a plan based on the Greek cross, with five domes. It was to be simplified internally by removing the bell-towers. According to his dynamic vision of the construction, the element which should be aimed at drawing the visitor to God was the Dome, to which he paid the greatest attention.

Only the drum had been completed in 1564, when Michelangelo died. Vignola then took over, and made no alternations to the plan; finally the dome was completed in the years 1586 to 1593 by Giacomo della Porta, who had the happy inspiration of raising the curve of the dome by eight metres, thus increasing the slope of the curves. Together with Fontana, he also built the lantern.

In the following years, a competition was held for extending the plan of the Basilica, again transforming it into a Latin Cross, at the wish of the Commission of Cardinals, and of Pope Paul V himself. In 1606 Carlo Maderno won this competition , with a project which provided for the broadening of the façade of the Basilica, with an external architrave surmounted by a low attic, and by statues, so as not to hide the view of Michelangelo's Dome. He extended the atrium, providing it with the five doors corresponding to the five naves of the church. Internally he adopted the scheme of the Latin Cross which was demanded by the needs of the liturgy; to Michelangelo's nave he added three new arches with lateral chapels. Maderno's work was severely criticised; however, we have to recognise that faced with the hard task of modifying Michelangelo's plan, he adopted the most sensitive and the most honest solution.

On 18th November 1626, after one hundred and twenty years of work, the new Basilica of Saint Peter's was consecrated by Pope Urban VIII. The thirteen hundredth anniversary of the first consecration of the ancient Basilica of Constantine fell on that day. The whole area which the ancient church had occupied was only the equivalent in space of the three naves of the 'extension made under the Borghese Pope, Paul V, whose name stands out on the architrave at the centre of the dedicatory inscription.

Statues of Popes and Saints around the attic of the colonnade of Piazza San Pietro

THE PIAZZA

When Bernini turned his attention to planning the reconstruction of Piazza San Pietro, in the early stages he envisaged a plan on a trapezoidal basis, but later he returned to the oval design first put forward by Rainaldi.

In this plan there were very specific considerations both of a spiritual and a psychological kind. The artist took full account of the surrounding buildings, such as the Apostolic Palaces, Maderno's fountain, the obelisk and the facade of the Basilica itself.

It was inevitable that the piazza should share in the mystical atmosphere surrounding the whole place, and for this reason the symbolic concept played an underlying role in the architectural planning. The idea of an all-embracing invitation to all Christians was envisaged by Bernini in its fullest sense, but it was filtered through the medium of the art of this period, taking conscious account of what had been done by Bernardo Rossellino at Pienza and Michelangelo in the Piazza del Campidoglio in Rome. These works take us into the study of perspective in the scenic planning of public squares, which sometimes reaches the level of illusionism.

Bernini intended to resolve the problem which presented itself to him in a manner in which architecture was conceived in both natural and allegorical terms. One of his drawings, unsigned, gives us a good idea of what was in the mind of the Pope who commissioned the work, Alexander VII, and of the artist himself: the Basilica is portrayed symbolically in this drawing by a man, possibly Saint Peter himself, whose head corresponds with the Dome of Michelangelo; he stretches out long arms - i.e. the two semicircles representing the arcades which were to be constructed, and he is welcoming and gathering to himself the faithful who are assembling to move into the Basilica.

In reconstructing the Piazza in front of the Basilica, Bernini first made a close study of the broad façade by Maderno and of the Dome, and then he conceived the idea of two semi-circles which would be linked by a rectangular area; thus the colonnade would relate more directly to the extended breadth of the façade and bestow on it some of the harmony which was in fact lacking.

In the Piazza, which is 240 metres (about 780 feet) wide, the colonnade, which was started in 1656 and completed in 1667, is made up of 284 Tuscan pillars, and 88 pilasters in travertine. The pillars taper slightly in the upper part, while the bulging effect known as *entasis* is noticeable. The columns and pilasters are grouped in four ranks which form three semicircular galleries; the largest gallery has a barrel-vaulted roof, while the two smaller side galleries, only 2.90 metres wide, have caisson ceilings.

At the internal end of the right-hand semi-circle of the colonnade is the Bronze Gateway - the main entrance to the Papal palace.

Above the columns there is a denticulated trabeation in the Ionic style, on which there are richly decorated pinnacles and the attic balustrade which joins the bases of the 162 statues of saints - most of them carved by Bernini's students under his personal direction. Corresponding to the beginning of the semicircular arcades, at the far end of the pediment, above the central gallery, are the arms of Alexander VII.

The obelisc at the centre of the Piazza - Egyptian, but devoid of hieroglyphic inscriptions - is a monolyth of pink granite, 25 metres high (82 ft), and weighing 440 tons. It was brought to Rome from Heliopolis in 37 A.D., on the orders of the Emperor Caligula, who had it erected in the Circus which he planned (and which was

Swiss Guards on Parade in St Peter's Square

afterwards called the Circus of Nero) - beside which the Basilica of Saint Peter would eventually be built. It was placed on a pedestal 15.5 metres high, supported by four bronze astragals. In the Middle Ages it was believed that at the summit of the huge monolith there had once been a golden urn containing the ashes of Julius Caesar, Augustus and Tiberius. It was still lying in its old place, where the Sacristy of St Peter's would later stand, until 1586, when it was transported to the centre of the Piazza by Domenico Fontana, and raised there on the spot on 10th September. The process of transportation took four months altogether, and 900 men, 150 horses and 47 winches were employed. A story which became legendary was that of the Liguran sailor Domenico Bresca; during the very dangerous operation of raising the obelisc, when he saw that the cables were burning because of the friction, he broke the ban on even the slightest sound which had been imposed by the pope (on pain of death) during the operation, and cried out 'Aigua ae corde', Genovese for 'Water on the Ropes!', and thus prevented a catastrophe. A replica of the Cross was placed at the summit of the obelisc, and bronze lions were substituted for the astragals at the base. Subsequently the meridian and the compass of winds were placed here, radiating from the base of the obelisc.

Both the fountains in the Piazza are supplied from Lake Bracciano by way of Trajan's aquaduct. The right hand fountain was originally placed in the Piazza under Innocent VIII in 1490, and then stood in a different position from its present one, somewhat asymmetrically. It was made up of a base with a round bath on top of it; above this was a carved basin and then another, smaller bath decorated with cupids. It was from this bath that the water flowed. This was demolished by Carlo Maderno in 1613 on the orders of Paul V, and when it was rebuilt, the small upper basin was reversed, and water flowed from it through seven spouts.

The second fountain, similar to the first, is the work of Bernini, and was erected under Innocent XI in 1677 after a long delay caused by difficulties in ensuring the necessary supply of water.

The staircase which leads up to the Basilica - similar in structure and conception to the 'Cordonata' of the Campidoglio - is based on a design by Michelangelo; at the foot of the staircase, on either side, there stand

The Archway of the Bells

Piazza San Pietro. In the foreground Carlo Maderno's fountain, 1613. ▶

VS PONT MAX AN MDC

Valadier's Clock (18th century), on the façade of the Basilica of St. Peter's.

statues of St. Peter and St. Paul. These were made in 1838 by G. Fabris and A. Tadolini for the Basilica of St. Paul's-without-the-Walls which was then being rebuilt, but in 1847 Pius IX ordered that they should be placed where they now stand, substituting them for much older ones which were attributed to Mino Da Fiesole and Paolo Romano.

In the façade of the Basilica, Carlo Maderno was almost reverentially respectful to Michelangelo's original concept, while giving the architectural composition more of a pictorial and decorative character. Michelangelo had envisaged the façade as completely subordinate to the Dome, setting aside the characteristic Renaissance preoccupation with the façade as such. Carlo Maderno, on the other hand, viewed the prospect as the expression of that typically Mannerist search for spatial effects, of which he had provided a prime example in the use of columns and loggias on the façade of Santa Susanna. The façade presents an essentially horizontal perspective: it is 114.69 metres (376 feet) long, and 45.44 metres (149 ft) high. There are eight massive columns, four pilasters and six half pilasters, all of the Corinthian order. Between them there are nine loggias, the central one being the loggia used for Papal benedictions. The body of this façade is extended beyond the width of the church itself, with two great archways leading out of the precinct; the one on the left, called the Arco delle Campane (The Arch of the Bells) leads in to the Piazzetta della Sagrestia.

Above the façade itself there is a trabeation surmounted by an undecorated further storey; at the far end of this storey and the balustrade which crowns it, corresponding to the central loggia, is a tympanum.

The great statues, each of them over 18 ft., which decorate this balustrade, portray the Redeemer (in the centre) flanked by John the Baptist and eleven of the Apostles (the missing one is St Peter, who is to be found at the foot of the staircase); the two eighteenth century clocks, made by Joseph Valadier at the request of Pius VI, correspond in position to the first and last of the loggias.

The Atrium of the Church is entered through five openings which correspond to the five doors of the Basilica.

THE ATRIUM

The Atrium - 71 metres long, 13.5 metres wide and 20 metres high (approximately 230 ft x 44 ft x 65 ft) - is a magnificent and noble monument to the religious taste of the seventeenth century in church decoration. **(1).**

The pavement was remodelled in 1888 under Leo XIII; it replaced the one based on the design by Bernini. The vault, supported by twenty marble columns in various colours, is given added splendour by the decorations in yellow stucco, showing scenes from the Acts of the Apostles - the work of Ambrogio Buonvicino. Dominating the scene is the coat of arms of Paul V Borghese.

The walls of the Atrium are divided by the six pilasters and by Ionic colums, and above the entrances and the doors there are tympanums in which can be seen the heads of the Cherubim carved by Borromini when he was still young. Between the doorways there are vaious important inscriptions At the top of the walls and the beginning of the vaulted ceiling are the lunettes containing the busts of thirty two martyred and canonised Popes.

Five doors lead from the Atrium into the Basilica; the two at the far sides give access to the lesser naves and the three central ones to the great central nave. From the left the first is the work of Manzù **(2)** in which the fully developed late vision of the artist can be seen: the theme is the Ascension of Christ and the Assumption of

Atrium of the Basilica

the Virgin. It is executed in a style which could be described as a refined form of classicism. The second door **(3)** is the Door of Good and Evil, the work of Luciano Minguzzi. The third door is the 'Porta Mediana' **(4)**, commissioned by Eugenius IV from Antonio Averulino, known as 'Il Filarete'; it dates from 1445. It is the work of a Florentine humanist, and its character is essentially a narrative one, the work of an artist who was steeped in the classics. Originally the door was three and a half metres wide and six metres high, but it was enlarged in 1619 so as to fit the new Basilica. The carved figures are in bronze; the freize around the panels is made up of mythological elements - animals, fruit, etc. The larger panels have reliefs with Christ, the Blessed Virgin, St. Paul and St. Peter, before whom the Pope (Eugenius IV) is portrayed kneeling; others show the martyrdom of the two 'Princes of the Apostles'. The lesser panels portray events concerning the pontificate of Eugenius IV, such as the Emperor John VIII Palaeologos in audience with the Pope; the same Emperor at the Council of Florence, the coronation of the (western) Emperor Sigismund of Luxembourg, and the handing over of the formularies of the faith to the Embassy from Abyssinia. In the internal part the story is told of the return of Filarete to the city riding on a donkey, in the midst of a crowd of disciples: this scene provides the work with a highly original 'signature'. Above the doorway is a bas-relief of Saint

The Gate of Death, by Giacomo Manzù

The Door of Good and Evil, by Luciano Minguzzi

Basilica of St. Peter's - the Holy Door, seen from the outside (above) and the inside (below)

Peter receiving the flock of Christians from Jesus - a work attributed to Bernini.

The fourth door **(5)**, the work of Venanzo Crocetti, is — like the work of Manzù — the product of the artist's own internal meditation, and it deals with the Seven Sacraments. The fifth and last door **(6)**, at the right, is the Porta Sancta; it is walled up, but is opened personally by the Pope every Holy Year. In the Jubilee of 1950 Swiss Catholics donated a bronze door with scenes inspired by the 'Grand Pardon', the work of Vico Consorti. This was placed at the reverse side of the Porta Sancta, inside the Basilica. Above the central entrance of the Atrium, opposite Filarete's door, is the mosaic of the 'Navicella' **(7)** the work of Giotto.This was commissioned from the painter by Cardinal Jacopo Gaetano Stefaneschi in 1298; it was formerly in the portico of the old basilica, and after the destruction of the latter it was housed in various places until Alexander VII (Chigi) had it placed in its present position. But the mosaic, because of the numerous restorations it has undergone, has lost a great deal of its original character. The scene of Christ walking on the water and calming the fears of the unbelieving Saint Peter, is linked in concept to Byzantine ideas, but the mode of expression is original and far more fluid.

The Atrium, with all its variety of different structural and ornamental elements, still presents a homogeneous and organic whole; in conceptual terms it is not so far distant from the proper funcion of the original square portico of the ancient basilica. At the two far ends, two great doorways lead into the lateral extensions through passageways which cut across the external arches; the Atrium thus extends for the whole length of the façade and it is prolonged on the right hand side as far as the Scala Regia itself, thus putting the Basilica into direct communication with the Papal Palace.

At the far end on the right is the statue of Constantine **(8)** by Bernini (1654-70, standing in a huge space. With this statue, the baroque tendency towards fluidity in sculpture finds a stage-setting in relation to the backdrop, a curtain of painted plasterwork, and the horse which is leaping out from it. At the other extreme is the statue of Charlemagne **(9)** on horseback, by Cornacchini (1725) against a mosaic background by P. Adami.

Interior of the Vatican Basilica

THE INTERIOR

The interior of the Basilica, in the form of a Latin cross, gives the initial impression, at least in the area preceding the dome, of being one vast nave, so that the two side-aisles which flank it, extended in their turn by side chapels, pass almost unnoticed. This architectural scheme, put into effect by Maderno on the basis of the lines laid down by the Council of Trent, is completed by the decoration added by Bernini; it makes use of a huge space while at the same time maintaining the unity of the whole interior.

The impression of unlimited size is provided not only by the dimensions but also by the fact that the main nave is in line with the internal pilasters of the Dome, and carries on all the way from the entrance at the same width, 25 metres, as far as the apse. The length overall is 186.36 metres.

The side-aisles which are c.20 feet wide, are only 250ft long, and end at the pilasters of St Longinus and St Andrew, opening into the great square into which the circle of the Dome is inserted. From this square, the three apses begin, which form the head of the Latin cross around the dome. If we can imagine the Redeemer stretched out on this enormous cross, we see that its central point, with the altar and the Confessio, lies at the point where his heart would be.

The perfect harmony of the architectural decoration is also achieved by keeping the main nave entirely free of altars and monuments — these are placed in the side aisles and in the chapels and along the walls of the transept and the apse. The only projection from the line of the pilasters is the bronze statue of St Peter, which we shall examine later. There are in all 45 altars, 25 monuments and 11 chapels; 10 minor domes. For a planned visit we may divide these up into five groups (see plan on page 6)

At the beginning of our tour, we should take an overall

look at the main nave **(10)** with its four arcades supported by pillars in pairs with pilaster strips, and with its splendid caisson roof vault, with the gilded ribbing. The massiveness of the pillars is somewhat lightened in the upper part by niches with statues of the Holy Founders of Religious Orders. The two gigantic holy water stoups, **(11)** the work of Agostino Cornacchini, are attached to the two first pillars; they date from the early eighteenth century: huge cherubs carved by Francesco Moderati hold marble shells in antique yellow, with grey marble draperies designed by Giuseppe Lironi.

The figures are shown on the pavement for the length of the world's largest churches: but a much more significant historical curio is the large disc in red porphyry **(12)** brought here from the ancient basilica, where it once stood before the high altar; on this disc — the *rota porphyretica* — more than twenty emperors; from Charlemagne to Frederick II, were crowned by the Popes.

Right-hand nave

Our journey begins with the right nave **(13)**, corresponding to the Porta Sancta, above which is the mosaic of St Peter **(14)**, the work of Ciro Ferri (1675). the roof of the side aisles is formed by three oval domes, one for each of the bays to which the side-chapels open.

The first chapel is the famous one containing the *Pietà* **(15)** — this chapel also has an oval dome as a roof, with frescos painted by Giovanni Lanfranco, representing the Triumph of the Cross, and angels holding the symbols of the Passion. The theme of the whole decoration is the salvation of mankind achieved by the sacrifice of Christ; Michelangelo's *Pietà* also belongs to this strain of devotion. It was commissioned from the artist by Cardinal Jean de Villier in 1498, when the artist was only twenty five and had recently arrived in Rome.

The marble group of the Pietà has a symbolic quality, for it combines a human theme with a divine vision. It is a

Holy Water Stoup by Agostino Cornacchini, with the huge cherubs by Francesco Mochi

remodelling in the artistic language of the fifteenth century Renaissance of a subject which already existed in the iconography of the Gothic tradition. In this work, the pyramidal construction typical of Leonardo is the basis of the structure, but it is executed in such a way that there are memories of the Gothic style in evidence as well. However, the model has its own absolute individuality based on a neo-Platonic vision of a work of art. The Madonna who is of huge proportions because she is able to receive in her lap not only Christ but the whole of suffering humanity, shows an intentional disproportion between the head and the body: the face, lovingly modelled in the finest detail, shows the traditional purity of the Virgin whose conception was without original sin. Closed in her silent sorrow, she cradles the naked body of Christ in her folds of her clothing; the beautifully moulded lines of his body are sublime, and show no sign of the martyrdom of the Cross; his death is signalled only by

Michelangelo's Pietà

the abandonment of the way in which he is laid in his mother's mantle — almost an ideal return to the maternal lap.

As we move down the right aisle, we have the monument to Queen Christina of Sweden (1625 to 1689); this was completed in 1702 by Giovanni Theudon and Lorenzo Ottoni to a design by Carlo Fontana **(16).** In the bas-relief the Queen is shown at the moment of her conversion to Catholicism in the Cathedral of Innsbruck in 1655. Opposite is the monument to Pope Leo XII (Della Genga) 1823-1829, represented as he gives the 'Urbi et Orbi' benediction during the Jubilee Year of 1825: among the cardinals who are portrayed at the scene is Mauro Cappellari, who was to become Pope under the name of Gregory XVI, and who commissioned this work in 1836 from G. Fabris **(17).** Below is the entrance to the Chapel of St Nicholas of the Crucifix **(18)**, designed by Bernini on an oval plan. Many relics are preserved here, and there is a wooden crucifix attributed to Cavallini, which was in the ancient Basilica, on the altar of St Simon and St Jude. The Chapel is closed to the public because the lift by means of which the Pope comes down to the Basilica is situated here.

The following chapel is that of St Sebastian **(19)**, which takes its name from the large mosaic of P. Cristofari (1738) which reproduces the original one by Domenichino, showing the martyrdom of the saint. Beneath the altar is the body of Innocent XI, which was brought here after his beatification. On the right hand side of the chapel is the monument to Pius XI **(20)**, the Pope of the Reconciliation with Italy, and of Catholic Action (1922 to 1939); it is the work of Pietro Canonica. Opposite is the monument to his successor Pius XII, **(21)** the Pope of the second world war (1939 to 1958), by F. Messina. The decorations of the dome are closely related in content to the subject of the mosaic.

The monument of Innocent XII is on the right **(22)** and opposite this is the memorial to Countess Matilda of Canossa.

The Marble group of the papal monument, in high baroque style (F. Valle and F. Fuga) shows the Pope seated on a throne between Charity and Justice. The monument to Matilda of Canossa **(23)** was first designed by Bernini in 1635, and completed in 1637. In a perspective arch, the statue of the Countess is placed with a sceptre in her right hand and the keys and the Papal crown in the left, symbolising the defence of the Papacy. Matilda of Tuscany was in fact the ruler who strongly upheld Gregory VII in the Investiture Conflict with the Empire in the eleventh century. On the funerary urn — the first containing a woman's body to be placed in this basilica, is a bas-relief by Stefano Speranza, showing the humbling of the Emperor Henry IV at Canossa.

The Chapel of the Most Holy Sacrament **(24)** closed by an iron grille by Francesco Borromini, has decorations which allude to the Eucharistic Mystery. On the altar is the sumptuous tabernacle in gilded bronze, designed by Bernini, in which the design of the little church of St Peter in Montorio by Bramante is re-presented in baroque form. The columns of the Tabernacle are ornamented by lapis-lazuli, the trabeation is crowned with small statues of the Apostles, and the tiny dome with a statue of Christ; at the sides are two adoring angels. The altarpiece representing the Holy Trinity is the work of

Michelangelo's Pietà - The Head of Christ

G. Theudon and L. Ottani: Monument to Christina of Sweden (1702)

Pietro da Cortona, while on the altar at the right is a mosaic copy of a painting by Domenichino showing the Ecstasy of St Francis.

Beyond the Sacrament Chapel is the monument to Gregory XIII (1572-1585) in white marble, carved by G. Rusconi in 1723. **(25)**. The Pope is portrayed between the symbols of Religion and Magnificence; the sarcophagus on which the statue rests has reliefs which recall the reform of the Julian Calendar by Gregory XIV - the Pope who succeeded Sixtus V for less than one year (**26**). The marble urn is flanked by the two statues of Religion and Justice, by P. Antiche.

At the end of this aisle, backing on to one of the pillars supporting the Dome, is the altar with the mosaic of the Communion of Saint Jerome (**27**), from a painting by Domenichino which is today in the Vatican Art Gallery.

The right wing of the transept (28)

The first chapel in the Transept is the Gregoriana **(29)** which reflects in its dome (one of the four surrounding the great Dome) the geometrical concept which Michelangelo had of spatial dimensions. It was he who began it, and Giacomo della Porta, following the Master's plans, completed it. The name comes from Pope Gregory XIII, during whose Pontificate it was completed (1583). It is enriched with a remarkable variety of plaster carvings, mosaics and precious marbles, in the taste of tha era. The altar, which is particularly splendid with marbles and semiprecious stones, has the image of the Madonna del Soccorso dating from the eleventh century, brought here by Gregory XIII after having stood for many centuries in the ancient basilica. Beneath this altar, one of the seven Marian altars in the Basilica, are the remains of Saint Gregory Nazianzen.

In the interior of the Chapel, on the right -hand side, is

De Fabris: Monument to Leo XII (1836)

the monument to Gregory XVI (1831-1846), the work of a neo-classical artist, Luigi Amici **(30)**. In a niche supported by four columns of ancient grey marble, the Pope is represented seated on his throne, with Wisdom and Prudence beside him; the sarcophagus below has scenes illustrating his labours for the spread of the Faith.

In the passage between the pillar of the dome and right wing of the transept is the tomb of the Lambertini Pope, Benedict XIV (1740-1758) by Pietro Bracci **(31)** This Pope, shown in the act of blessing the faithful for the Jubilee of 1750, is flanked by the two statues of Wisdom and Impartiality, the work of Gaspare Sibilla. Opposite is the altar of Saint Basil the Great **(32)**, on which a mosaic originating from the painting by Soubleyras (1745) shows the Emperor Valens fainting with emotion during the Mass celebrated by St Basil.

From this point we come into the right wing of the transept, **(33)** and the great "Crossing" planned by Michelangelo is shown in all its huge and masterly proportions. The vault is decorated with fine stucco work: in three roundels there are events from the Lives of the

P.S. Mannot: Tomb of Innocent XI

G.L. Bernini: Monument to Matilda of Canossa (1635-37). On the funerary vase is a bas-relief by Stefano Speranza with the humilitation of the Emperor Henry IV at Canossa.

Apostles taken from the arrases by Raphael preserved in the Vatican. In the niches are more statues of founders of the Religious Orders. Three altars stand here: that of St Wenceslas, with three mosaics by Caroselli **(34)**, that of Sts. Processus and Marianus where the mosaics are copied from the originals by Jean de Boulogne **(35)** and that of Saint Erasmus, with mosaics from the originals by Nicholas Poussin **(36)**.

Continuing down the right hand side of the transept we find on the right the monument to Clement XIII (Rezzonico) (1758-1769) by Antonio Canova **(37)**. In this group there is a synthesis between the Hellenistic vision and that of the neo-classical period, in which the

G. Rusconi: Monument to Gregory XIII (1723)

Gian Lorenzo Bernini: The Throne of St. Peter ▶

idealisation of the subject does not exclude his individuality. Clement XIII is shown in the act of prayer, above a sarcophagus with Charity and Hope in bas-relief, while at the sides, the figures of the Genius of Death and Religion have two lions at their feet.

Opposite this stands the altar of the Navicella (little ship) **(38)**, so-called because of the subject of its mosaic, copied from a fresco by Giovanni Lanfranco (1582 to 1647). From here, we enter one of the chapels of Michelangelo **(39)**, the one with the altar of St Michael **(40)** which has a mosaic copy of the painting by Guido Reni, and the altar of St Petronilla **(41)** with a mosaic from a picture by Guercino, which is the largest altar-piece in the whole basilica.

East wall of the transept (42)

Beyond this Chapel, on the right, is the baroque tomb of Clement X (1670-1676) by Mattia de Rossi **(43)**. The Pope (in a statue by Ercole Ferrata) is seated between Clemency (by G. Mazzuoli) and Benificence (by L. Morelli).

Opposite, above an altar, is the mosaic showing St Peter raising Tabitha **(44)**. At this point we have reached the beginning of the apse **(45)**, to which we pass by means of two porphyry steps belonging to the old basilica. In this area, the luminous spaciousness of Michelangelo's concept meets with the baroque triumph of the Cathedra of St Peter **(46)** by Bernini. This work was commissioned by Pope Alexander VI Chigi, (1655-1667) in order to surround the bronze and gold casing covering the wooden throne with ivory decorations said to be that of St Peter himself. The plan of composition, which belongs more to the field of sculpture than of architecture, is derived from the painting of the Circumcision of Christ by Rubens , but on a completely symbolic and scenographical plan.

The huge gilded bronze complex is thus seen from the main entrance to the Basilica as virtually enclosed perspectively in the columns of the Baldacchino, in a vision of theatrical grandeur. The nucleus of the whole work is a glazed oval window, surrounded by angels who lean out from it, while those below move towards the exterior in the midst of a myriad rays of golden light. The huge Cathedra, between two columns of precious marble, is supported by four gigantic figures in rich draperies (each of them more than five metres high), representing the Doctors of the Church - the Westerners Ambrose and Augustine in front and the Easterners, Athanasius and

Altar of Saint Jerome, with a mosaic reproduction by Cristofari of Domenicho's St. Jerome, now in the Vatican Gallery.

GNOS
ΣΥ ΒΟΣΚΕΙΣ

John Chrysostom behind, all standing on great pedestals of marble.

At either side of the apse there are two funerary monuments; to the right, the one to Urban VIII Barberini, (1624-44) by Gian Lorenzo Bernini, and on the left the one to Paul III Farnese (1534-1549), the work of Guglielmo della Porta, under the direction of Michelangelo.

The tomb of Urban VIII **(47)** was ordered by the Pope himself in 1628, but it was only concluded in 1647. This sepulchre is the prototype of all the other baroque tombs which were to follow, with its pyramidal design, the vividness of the portrayal of the Pope, and the naturalism of the two statues which flank him — Charity and Justice — which are not at all symbolic, but unreservedly feminine. Contrasting with this is the winged skeleton on the urn itself, the only thing which brings to mind the idea of death.

The monument to Paul III **(48)**, placed like its counterpart in a large niche, has echoes in the symbolism of Justice and Prudence and in the geometrical arrangement of the figures, of what Michelangelo had designed for the Sagrestia Nuova of San Lorenzo in Florence. But in the arrangement we see now, composed by Bernini, the monument has lost the other two allegorical statues of Peace and Abundance, while the superb nude of Justice was covered with a drape by Bernini himself.

From the apse, we interrupt our tour round the edge of the church and approach the corner of the Cathedra of St Peter in order to stand right in the centre of the church, where the great Baldacchino of G. L. Bernini stands, 29 metres (95 feet) in height, **(49)** directly beneath the dome, and directly above the Papal altar. It was commissioned in 1624 by Urban VIII, Barberini. It was finally consecrated in 1633 (28th June) by the same Pope.

Bernini approached this work keenly aware of the environment into which it had to be fitted, and with a constant interest which kept him busy with the task for a good ten years. He conceived the idea of a baldacchino in which the plastic arts would have a more important role than the architectural design, through a personal vision of a pictorial kind. It would take its inspiration from those "artificiosissime macchine" which were among the technical means used by the theatre of which Bernini was a devotee, and thus for the papal altar he envisaged a baldacchino similar to those which were carried during pageants and processions. His structures are not confined to the space in which they actually stand; they swirl freely out of them; the four columns obtained from the bronzes of the pro-naos of the Pantheon have a spiral shape; they are twined with laurel sprays, from which gracious little cherubs peer out, and above the columns, four angels hold up, by means of cords, drapes on which appear the Barberini bees. The crowning section is in the shape of a diadem with four curved ribs, united at the top by a globe surmounted by the Cross; the arms of the Barberini, with the three bees, can be seen in the space between two of the ribs, facing the main entrance. Despite its rich decoration, the baldacchino, with its sinu-

Gian Lorenzo Bernini: Monument to Urban VIII (1628-47)

Guglielmo della Porta: Monument to Paul III

G. L. Bernini: The Baldacchino

S·PETRI GLORIAE SIXTVS PP·V·A·M·D·XC·PONTIF·V·

Upper part of Bernini's Baldacchino and interior of the dome.

Francesco Mochi: The Veronica. The niche is hollowed out of the pillar which stands above the spot where Julius II laid the first foundation stone of the new Basilica.

Francesco Duchesnoy: Saint Andrew

G.L. Bernini: Saint Longinus

ous curves and its gilded bronze colour, in no way damages the grave simplicity of the architecture of Michelangelo which surrounds it.

Beneath the Baldacchino is the Papal Altar — so called because only the Pope may celebrate Mass on it. This altar surrounds the ancient ones of St Gregory the Great and St Calixtus II. It stands above the Confessio **(50)**, the subterranean chapel built by Maderno and reached by means of two marble staircases, in which 89 branch candlesticks of gilded bronze hold the vast number of bulbs illuminating the tomb of Peter.

The Baldacchino, the Altar and the Confessio stand immediately under the enormous dome of Michelangelo, which rests on four gigantic pilasters marking out the central crossing. On the inner sides are four niches each ten metres high, built by Bernini. In these there are several statues, 5 metres high — that of St Longinus **(55)**, the soldier who pierced the side of Christ with his lance, which is the work of Bernini himself; that of St Helena, mother of Constantine **(52)**, who brought the relics of the true cross to Rome in the fourth century — this is the work of Andrea Bolgi; that of Veronica **(53)**, who according to legend wiped the face of Christ during his journey to Calvary — by Franceso Mochi (it should be noted that the pillar of Veronica stands exactly at the point where Julius II laid the first stone for the new basilica). The last statue is that of St Andrew **(54)** by Francois Duchesnoy.

Above the niches are Bernini's four loggias, each of them decorated with two marble columns from the old basilica. From these loggias are exposed the reliquaries of the Sacred Lance, the fragment of the True Cross, preserved in a cross "of the bees"; the "Holy Face" of Veronica's cloth, and the head of St Andrew the Apostle.

As we look at the pilaster of St Longinus, immediately to the right is the greatly venerated statue of St Peter **(56)**, which according to an ancient legend was made from the bronze of the statue of Capitoline Jove, and cast on the orders of Pope Leo I after he had stopped Attila, as a thank-offering. This, however, is a legend which is very doubtful from the chronological standpoint, as indeed is the traditional attribution of the statue to Arnolfo di Cambio (thirteenth century).

The Saint is portrayed seated on a marble chair (dating from the Renaissance), with a severe expression, but in the act of benediction. The whole work is placed on a pedestal by C. Marchionni (1756-57), in Sicilian jasper with green porphyry decorations.

In 1857 Pius IX had granted an Indulgence of 50 days to all those who kissed the foot of this ancient statue with devotion; it was the same Pope who, in 1871, ordered the making of a background mosaic in imitation of a brocade. This is in fact in rather strident colours, but it fits well with the rich robes with which the figure is vested on St Peter's Day. Pius IX is also remembered in the mosaic medallion above the statue, as the first Pope to exceed the twenty-five years of rule as Pontiff attributed to St Peter. His reign in fact lasted 32 years, from 1846 to 1878. At the foot of the statue, there are two candlesticks in figured bronze, fine examples of modern workmanship.

Turning towards the apse and resuming our course, we see the monument to Alexander VIII (1689-1691) by Arrigo di San Martino **(57)**, with the figures of Religion and Prudence in white marble, and the bas-relief at the base of the statue by Angelo De Rossi (1751). Opposite is the altar of the Healing of the Paralytic by St Peter, with a mosaic altar-piece from a drawing by F. Mancini **(58)**

Bronze statue of St. Peter, attributed to Arnolfo di Cambio (13th century)

The left-hand side of the transept (59)

In the corner between the side of the rear portion and the left-hand side of the Transept is the third of Michelangelo's Chapels, known as the Chapel of the Column **(60)**, in the dome of which, between angels and festoons, are the symbols of the Litany of Loreto. The altar opposite has an image of the Madonna painted on a column of the central nave of the old basilica.

Below the altar are the remains of Popes Leo II, III and IV, while beneath the pavement Leo XII (Della Genga) is buried. At the left is the altar of St Leo the Great **(61)**, with the remains of the Pope, who stopped the *flagellum dei,* Attila the Hun, as portrayed in a large bas-relief by Alessandro Algardi (1650).

From the corner Chapel of the Column, we have now moved into the left hand wing of the transept, where the first monument to catch our eye, on the right, is that to the Chigi Pope, Alexander VII, 1655-1667, the work of Bernini and his pupils **(62)**. The Pontiff is portrayed between Justice, Prudence, Charity and Truth; a skeleton is raising a drape made of Sicilian jasper. This was the original solution which Bernini found for arranging this monumental tomb around an already existing door, which gives access to the Chapel of St Martha. Opposite is the altar with the mosaic of the Sacred Heart of Jesus, by C. Muccioli **(63)**. From this altar we move into the body of the left wing of the Transept **(64)** with its vault decorated by Vanvitelli and with plasterwork decorations by Maini showing scenes from the life of Peter. There are three altars: St Thomas **(65)** with a mosaic by Vincenzo Camuccini; St Joseph **(66)**, with a painting by A. Funi, and the Crucifixion of St Peter, **(67)** with a mosaic taken from an original by Guido Reni.

In the area beside the pillar of St Andrew, there is the Altar of the Lie **(68)** on the left (so called because of its mosaic based on a painting by Pomarancio showing the Punishment of Ananias and Sapphira, the married couple who lied to Peter). Opposite this is the cold, neo-classical monument to Pius VIII (1829-30) by Tenerani **(69)** overweight with sculpture and grimly academic in style. In the corner of the transept is the Michelangelo

Chapel known as the Clementina **(70)**, which was finished off by Giacomo della Porta. As we go in, the eye is caught by the arms of Clement VIII (1592-1605) in mosaic work, which are placed both on the pavement and on the dome. the pendentives have illustrations of the Doctors of the Church (both Latin and Greek) while in the lunettes are shown the Visitation, Saints Zacharias and Elizabeth, Daniel in the Lions' Den and Malachi helped by the Angel. The altar, consecrated in 1628, contains the remains of St Gregory the Great **(71)**. The fine altarpiece is taken from an original by Andrea Sacchi.

At the left is the memorial to Pius VII, **(72)**, which was put up by Cardinal Consalvi and made by Thorwaldsen. On either side of the Pope who is giving his blessing are two little allegorical representations of the Genii of Time and of History; lower down are Strength and Wisdom. The banal architectural background and the coldness of the sculptures make this one of the least successful and harmonious monuments in the basilica. Backing on to the pillar of St Andrew, at the end of the left-hand nave, is the Altar of the Transfiguration **(73)** with the enlarged mosaic copy of the masterpiece begun by Raphael in 1517, now in the Vatican Art Gallery.

Left-hand side aisle (74)

At this point we have begun the return journey down the side of the left-hand aisle. On the right is the monument to Leo XI Medici **(75)** by Alexander Algardi, all in white marble, showing the Pope standing between the statues of Prudence (by Ercole Ferrata) and Liberality (by Giuseppe Peroni), which are among the finest baroque allegorical works. Leo XI died in 1605 after an extremely brief pontificate — 27 days in all — and it is to this that the rosebuds allude, with their inscription Sic floruit - thus did he flourish. However as legate of Clement VIII, he had been a participant in a major event in history — the abjurations and submission of Henry IV of France, as shown on the funerary urn.

On the left is the tomb of Innocent XI (Odescalchi) (1676-89), by Petro Stefano Mannot, on a design by Carlo Maratti **(76)**, where the Pope is on the urn with personifications of Religion and Justice on either side. Immediately to the right is the Chapel of the Choir **(77)** closed by an iron grille by Borromini; on the oval dome are stucco scenes from the Old and New Testaments by G.B. Ricci of Novara, who worked under the guidance of G. Della Porta's drawings. A marble shield records that Clement XI is buried in a small area beneath the pavement: the lavabo basin has a large scene from the Apocalypse. Behind the altar, under which lie the remains of St John Chrysostom and relics of St Francis and St Anthony, is the mosaic of the Immaculate Conception, with Sts Francis, John Chrysostom and Anthony. The splendour of the ceiling contrasts with the austerity of the choir-stalls in dark wood, which create an atmosphere of deep mysticism suitable for the important liturgical functions which are performed here.

Immediately outside this Chapel on the right is the monument to St Pius X **(78)** by the sculptor Pier Enrico Astorri and the architect Florestano di Fausto. The statue of the Pope, standing, is placed in a niche: below are two reliefs with the Communion of the Children and the Homage of the Wise to Faith.

On the opposite side is the famous monument of Innocent VIII (1484-92), a splendid bronze work by

◀ *Altar of the Lie, with the mosaic showing the punishment of Ananias and Sapphira, from a painting by Pomarancio*

Gian Lorenzo Bernini: Monument to Alexander VII ▶

ALEXANDER·VII
CHISIVS
PONT·MAX

PONT OPT MAX

Antonio del Pollaiolo: Monument to Innocent VIII (1492) transferred here from the former basilica of St. Peter

Antonio Canova: Monument to the Stuarts

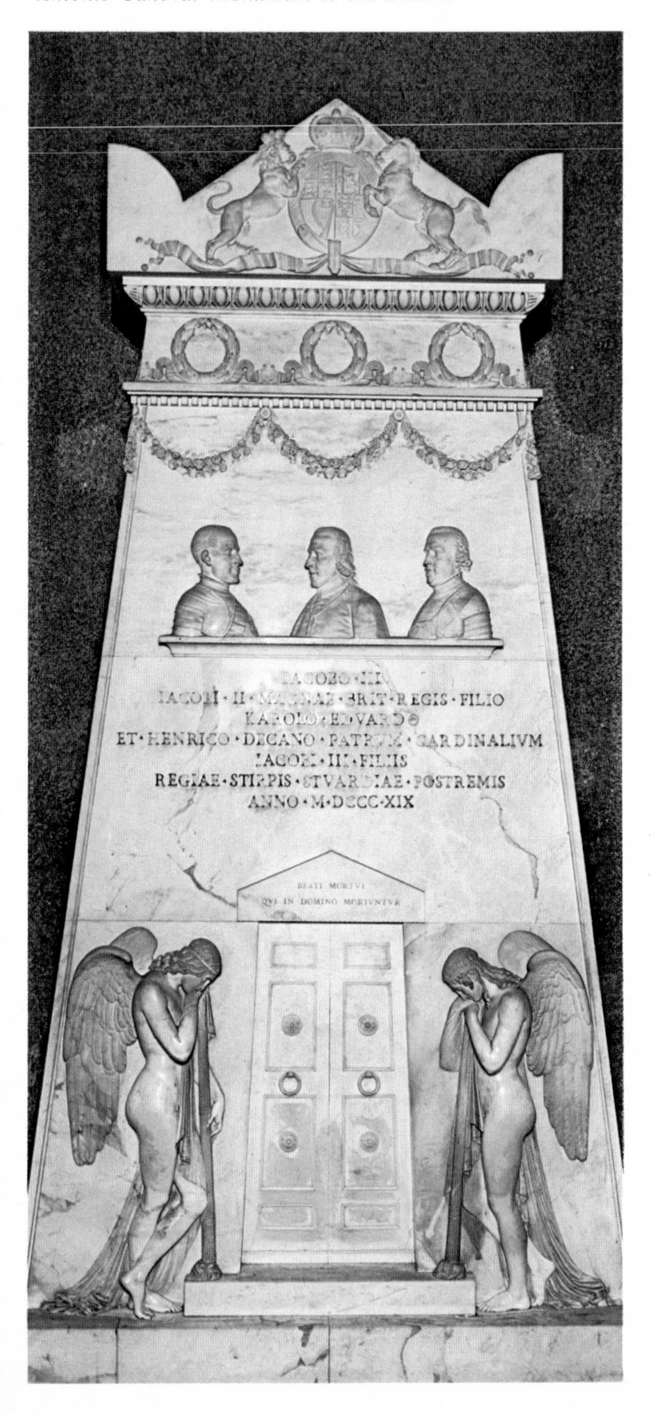

Antonio Pollaioulo, which is in the characteristic fifteenth century "pavilion" style of monumental tomb. **(79)**. The Pope is portrayed twice; lying on the funeral casket in the sleep of death, and seated on his throne, surrounded by four bas-reliefs in which, framed by artificial niches, are the allegories of the four Cardinal Virtues. The monument was formerly in the ancient basilica, where it was dedicated in 1492; after being transferred to the new church it underwent a number of changes of place which altered its original appearance.

As we move forward on the right hand side, we find the Chapel of Mary known as the "Presentation", since the altarpiece is a mosaic taken from an original of that name by Romanelli, with the Presentation of the Blessed Virgin in the Temple **(80)**. Beneath the altar is the body of St Pius X. The vault of the chapel is painted with biblical scenes illustrating the pre-figuring of Mary in the Old Testament. At the right hand side of the altar is the provisional loculus,or burial niche, for the Popes, used before their final entombment. In this Chapel there are also monuments to Benedict XV, the work of Pietrò Canonica **(81)**, and John XXIII, by Emilio Grego **(82)**.

As we come back out, on the right hand side above the door which gives access to the staircase leading to the Dome, is the monument to Maria Clementina Sobieski, the wife of James Stuart (known to Jacobites as James III, and to others as the Old Pretender) **(83)**. Pietro Bracci carried out the sculptural work in 1745, on the basis of designs by Filippo Barigioni — Charity is shown holding up an oval disc with the portrait of the dead subject in mosaic, taken from a painting by Ignazio Sterne.

On the left hand side we see the funerary stele of the last Stuarts **(84)**, a work planned by Antonio Canova in 1817 but actually carried through in 1821 at the wish of the then king of England, George IV. In the two figures of the Genii of Death on either side of the symbolic door of the sepulchre Christian mysticism does not diminish the effect of copying exquisite forms of pagan work.

When we come to the Chapel of the Baptismal Font, we have reached the end of our tour of the interior of the Basilica. The dome of this Chapel,on the drum of which there are statues and angels, shows scenes representing the three types of Baptism: by water, by desire and by blood. The theme of the work in the lunettes and the pendentives is also connected with Baptism.

There are three large mosaics on the walls: the Baptism of Jesus in the centre, from a painting by Carlo Maratt; St Peter baptising Saints Processus and Marianus (by G. Passeri) on the right, and the Centurion Cornelius (By A. Procaccini) on the left. The shell of the Baptismal Font is the cover of a great porphyry sarcophagus, which according to tradition came from the Mausoleum of Hadrian, and was formerly in the Atrium of the ancient basilica, covering the tomb of Otto II. It was further decorated by Carlo Fontana with the upper section in bronze.

NT. MAX.
EGENERATIONIS
RITV INSTAVRA
SAL. MDCCX
SVI

THE DOME

The climb up to the Dome is a necessary complement to any visit to St. Peter's ; this alone, together with the rather difficult task of touring round the outside of the basilica, can give a direct vision of the architectural genius of Michelangelo in all its grandeur and purity, free from the embellishments and the impositions of later ages which abound in the interior. From the roof of the basilica, which is reached by a spiral staircase from the door in the left-hand side aisle, between the Chapel of the Presentation and that of the baptismal font, Michelangelo's dome can be seen in all its massiveness and its beauty. He conceived it in very different terms from those originally proposed by Bramante, similar to the dome of the Pantheon, resting on a large drum with windows from which project sixteen buttresses. Each buttress is marked out by a pair of columns with Corinthian capitals, and the whole section is crowned with a trabeation which does not run continously, but alternates between projecting and indented sections, similar to the one which the artist had painted many years earlier in the vault of the Sistine Chapel.

Above the drum soars the dome itself, resting on a base decorated with festoons, to lighten the enormous mass. Michelangelo makes use of the double casing, as Brunelleschi had done in Santa Maria de' Fiori in Florence. Externally, sixteen ribs project upwards from the buttresses, and these serve the double function of acting as a skeleton for the dome and accentuating the upward movement; they meet at the lantern where the motif of the pairs of projecting columns is repeated.

We could say that Michelangelo's Dome is the greatest architectural masterpiece of all time, and yet this marvellous work is incomplete, if we compare it with the wooden model preserved in the Vatican Museum, and faithfully reproducing the artist's actual scheme. We see in fact that the sixteen connecting spiral columns between the cornice of the drum and the cornice on which the dome rests — more than five metres high — were never built, nor were the statues which were supposed to be put up at the base of each of these volutes. It is clear that Della Ponta and Fontana, who completed the work on the dome, used the buttresses of the drum to put their scaffolding up, and once they had done so, they did not give another thought to the statues which were intended to crown the buttresses themselves.

When we go up from the roof of the basilica to the base of the drum — another marvellously scenic view spreads out from the balustrade which stands at a height of 53 metres (160 feet) from the pavement, towards the interior of the church. From here it is possible to enjoy a complete vision of Michelangelo's enormous 'crossing', of the pilasters which hold up the dome, and the three apsidal wings; in one glance one can take in the astonishing spatial proportions of the whole composition. From the same internal balustrade we get a good view of the mosaics which decorate the drum of the dome and the sections between the ribs of the inside canopy, where the Heavenly Courts are represented, and at the top, the Eternal Father: these were made to a design by the Cavalier Piero d'Arpino. Lower down in the four pendentives of the dome, the four Evangelists are portrayed, in roundels which are 8 metres (26 feet) wide.

The remainder of the ascent of the dome is made by climbing up long spiral corridors which are built in the intervening space between the inner and outer casings of the dome. When we come out on to the last circular terrace, at the external base of the lantern, we have before our eyes the most extensive and complete view over Rome, better than any plan or description can offer for those who wish to see something of the urban development of the City, the course of the River Tiber, and the pattern of the hills right up to the limits of the horizon. Nearer at hand, all around the church, can be seen the vaious parts of the Vatican City: St Peter's Square, the Audience Chamber, the Gardens, the Sistine Chapel, the Museum buildings with the great Belvedere Courtyard built by Bramante, and later divided into three parts by the New Wing and the Library.

The lantern imitates, and virtually reproduces, the architectural design of the drum, with buttresses and pairs of jutting columns, an irregular trabeation, and linking volutes similar to those built between the drum and the dome, and finally the crowning spire, ribbed and surmounted by the great ball in bronze with the Cross above it.

132.50 metres in height (435 feet) it is the highest dome ever built in masonry, but it is its solemn and harmonious nobility of style which makes it also the most beautiful dome in the world.

Chapel of the Baptismal Font. In the background the mosaic by Cristofari (1722) showing the Baptism of Jesus, from a painting by Carlo Maratti. In foreground, the baptismal font, the porphyry shell of which comes from the Mausoleum of Hadrian (Castel Sant'Angelo), and during the Middle Ages acted as a cover for the tomb of Otto II in the atrium of the ancient Basilica. The splendid bronze decoration is the work of Carlo Fontana

Basilica of St. Peter's - the Dome. ▶

THE SACRISTY AND THE TREASURY OF ST. PETER'S

The Sacristy is reached from the basilica through a door beneath the monument to Pius VIII. As it is a separate building, it is reached by means of a corridor.

The site of the Sacristy was not studied with great care by Maderno in relation to the whole structure of St. Peter's. It was only in 1776, when Pius VI was Pope, sixty one years after a previous competition which was won by Filippo Juvara, that the construction was finally begun, by C. Marchionni. This architect was adept at uniting decorative elaboration with a rational use of space, so that the building was designed to house the Common Sacristy, the Sacristy of the Canons, that of the Beneficed clergy, the Capitol, the Archives and the Treasury.

The first place that one sees is a circular vestibule with columns, in which there is a sixteenth century statue of St. Andrew, attributed to Paolo Romano. Two corridors then lead to the Common Sacristy, an octagonal room with eight fluted grey marble columns from the Villa of Hadrian, and a dome decorated with ceiling-roses and caissons. Set into the floor are the arms of Pius VI. The first door on the left leads into the Canons' Sacristy. On one door is a picture by Federico Zuccari showing the Glory of the Saints; in the Chapel which stands behind it are works by Francesco Penni — A Madonna and Child, Saint Anne, and Sts Peter and Paul — and by Giulio Romano (The Madonna, the Child Jesus and John Baptist); above the windows in the story of St. Peter, painted by Antonio Cavallucci.

The next room is that of the Capitol, with paintings by Andrea Sacchi representing St. Andrew, St. Veronica, St. Helena, St. Longinus and the Miracle of St. Gregory.

At the end of the corridor there is the entry to the Treasury of St. Peter. It was Constantine who began the practice of donating precious objects to St. Peter; he gave an altar of silver and gold with jewels. Theodosius I (379-95) and Honorius were particularly generous, but the invasion of Alaric and his Visigoths, the Vandals of Geneseric (455) and the Ostrogoths (546), after having seriously damaged the basilica, went on to despoil it of much of its treasure. However the spirit of the pilgrims and the faithful, allied to that of the Popes, united in restoring some of its riches.

Sixtus III (432-440), Hilarius (461-468), Symmachus (498-514) were very generous in their donations, and with Pelagius II (578-590) who decorated the Confessio with silver, Honorius I (625-638), John VII (705-707) who gave a chalice of gold studded with gems, and Gregory III (731-741) who decorated the basilica with onyx columns and many jewels, the Treasury of St. Peter reached an extremely high value. Hadrian I (771-793) kept up with the splendours of his predecessors by giving an enormous cross made of precious materials.

Dalmatic said to have belonged to Charlemagne

Contact with the barbarians produced gifts from some of their kings, such as Theodoric (two silver candlesticks) and Clovis (a gold crown studded with precious gems). At Christmas 800, Charlemagne offered Pope Leo III gold to replace the silver of the Confessio of St. Peter, but not to be outdone the Pope himself gave a gold statue of Christ and the twelve Apostles. Pope Pasqual I (817-824) was equally munificent.

However, during the sack of 846, the Saracens despoiled the basilica once again; Leo IV and his successor Benedict III immediately began the work of rebuilding the Treasure, but these efforts proved vain because of the arrival of the Normans under Robert Guiscard in 1084. It was Pope Urban II who began the rebuilding yet again.

The giving of precious objects reached a very high level much later on in history, when the Jubilee Years were instituted. The first, launched by Boniface VIII in 1300, brought the marks of devotion of thousands of humble pilgrims and rich members of the upper classes. Thus during the Avignon period, the Treasury was enriched by Urban VI (1362-70) by the busts of Sts Peter and Paul (the work of Giovanni di Bartolo) in silver and gold with precious stones. These were melted down much later on by Napoleon.

The period of the Renaissance saw the culminating point in the enrichment of the Treasury, both because of the skill of the goldsmiths of the Latium, and because of the goldsmiths' stalls which were situated in front of the basilica itself. In the later fifteenth century, the finest of craftsmen in metal came from Tuscany, such as Ghiberti, Brunelleschi and Verrocchio.

During the pontificates of Nicholas V (1447-55), Sixtus IV (1471-84), Leo X (1513-1521) and Clement VII (1523-34), the Treasury rose to an unprecedented splendour. Paul II (1464-1471) possessed a magnificent tiara, and an even more splendid one made by Ghiberti was owned by Eugenius IV (1431-47). When Rome was sacked by the imperial forces in 1527, it was an inexhaustible mine of booty.

In the seventeenth century, the presence of Gian Lorenzo Bernini as sculptor in the Vatican had a marked effect on the taste of work in gold and silver right through to the eighteenth century.

Even now, however, unhappy events were not at an end, and in the Napoleonic period Pius VI was forced to sacrifice part of the Treasure in order to meet the demands of the French. When this period had passed, the passion for rebuilding the Treasure was once more resumed, and this naturally meant that numerous neoclassical works were acquired.

During all these centuries, the gifts offered to the Treasury were not, of course, confined to jewels. We should mention the bronze candlesticks of Pollaiuolo, Cellini and Carlo Spagna — the latter based on designs by Bernini — and many masterpieces both of textile design and of embroidery, such as chasubles, stoles and copes, of which the finest examples belong to the Byzantine era and the Middle Ages.

Cross of Justin II

In the first Room, there are objects from the first basilica — one of the twelve vitineous columns in Parian

Bronze cockerel of the 9th century, from the ancient basilica

marble which were in the presbytery, and a gilded metal cockerel, dating from the eleventh century which once crowned the vane of the bell-tower.

Among the golden ornaments in the second Room, are the Cross of the Emperor Justin II of Constantinople (sixth century), which is still carried in procession during the Good Friday ceremonies, and a little cross with enamel inlays and six splendid pearls, encased in a reliquary in embossed workmanship, a marvellous Byzantine work of the sixth or seventh centuries. In the same room are the dalmatic said to belong to Charlemagne, the famous Ciborium of Donatello in sculpted marble, with the deeply venerated image of the Madonna della Febbre at its centre, and the copy of the wooden chair of St. Peter, the original of which, from the time of Charlemagne (9th century), has been incorporated into the 'Trionfo della Cattedra' by Bernini, in the apse of the basilica.

In the Third Room can be seen the bronze sepulchre of Sixtus IV (della Rovere) — somewhat akin to a monumental funeral couch; a very fine work in moulding and carved figures by Antonio del Pollaiuolo (1493), impregnated with the spirit of humanism both in its overall scheme and its details.

There are some reliquaries in the Fourth Room, among them a bust of St. Luke dating from the fourteenth century, while in the Fifth Room are several bronze candlesticks, finely modelled work of the sixteenth century; also two torchholders attributed to the school of Pollaiuolo. The Sixth Room has the statues of St. Peter and St. Paul in gilded bronze (16th century), a fifteenth century cross in rock crystal, some reliquaries, monstrances, and a great angel in clay by Bernini, which was used for the casting of one of the two angels placed at the sides of the Ciborium in the Chapel of the Most Holy Sacrament.

The Ninth Room is reserved for the Sarcophagus of Junius Bassus (fourth century), found in 1595 in the area of the Confessio. The decoration of the front section is divided up into ten scenes from the Old and New Testaments. On the smaller sides there are cherubs gathering the vintage (on the left) and the harvest (on the right).

Treasury of St. Peter's - Sarcophagus of Junius Bassus (4th cent.)

Vatican Caves - In the background, the niche of the Palliums, decorated with a mosaic

THE VATICAN CAVES

The 'Caves' of the Vatican were originally related to the work on the foundations of the ancient basilica, and then extended when the new one was built, as the floor was raised by three metres. Towards the end of the sixteenth century, Pope Gregory XIII had the Clementine peribolus around the outside of the semicircular crypt of the sixth century restored. The second part of the 'Caves' is made up of the 'Hypogean Hall' — the great subterranean area which was created as a result of the levelling work between the floor of the ancient basilica and that of the new one.

The Caves are divided into Old and New — the 'Grotte Vecchie' being the ones restored by Gregory XIII, which stretch out in three long corridors in the same direction as the naves of the Church, characterised by square pillars and a cross vault, while the 'Grotte Nuove' are beneath the Crossing and correspond to the Dome, spreading out into a semicircle.

The final systemisation of the Caves was carried out in 1939 and onwards, initially by order of Pius XI, who wanted to be buried near the tomb of St Pius X, which was actually in the Caves, but at a rather low point. These works of excavation led to the direct discovery of the Roman cemetery which lay below. Both the Old and New Caves now communicate with each other and make up a subterranean complex of considerable archaelogical and historical importance.

In the entrance rooms are some important finds from the Constantine basilica, and from the foundations of the Church itself; there are also the remains of the mosaic from the Chapel of Pope John VII (Room III),

The Vatican Confessio, with the Niche of the Palliums, over the tomb of St. Peter.

KA·BEATI·PETRI·CONF
A·PAVLO·PAPA·V·EIVS·SERV
EXORNATA
ANNO·DOM·MDCXV·PONT·XI

and Giotto's Angel (Room IV), which was part of the "Navicella' mosaic. Some statutes, such as the bust of Benedict XII by Paolo da Siena, were also appropriately placed in this atmosphere of suffused mysticism beneath the earth.

The New Caves are arranged around a narrow ambulatory.In this narrow walk are niches with statues of the Apostles. The decoration consists of fifteenth century bas-reliefs, mosaics, and above it all a low arched vaut which is also decorated. Along the passage there are chapels, such as that of Santa Maria delle Febbri, Santa Maria de Porticu, and finally the Chapel of the Confessio of St Peter. In this crypt chapel, everything is related to the Martyr himself, from the plan of the reversed cross to the bas-relief by G.B. Maini showing episodes in the life of St Peter and St Paul, and to the south-facing door behind which is the 'Red Wall'.

The Clementine peribolus leads to the Old Caves, which have a pavement in Travertine and another vaulted roof.

At the point where the right nave begins above, we find ourselves in the Chapel with the sarcophagus of Boniface VIII (1294-1303), the work of Arnolfo di Cambio, part of a sepulchral monument which, according to the wishes of the Pope himself, consisted of a funeral memorial enclosed in a chapel of the ancient basilica.

Next to the tomb of Boniface VIII are the sarcophagus of Nicholas III Orsini (1277-1280) and a very beautiful bas-relief with the Virgin, the Infant Christ, and the Apostles Peter and Paul.

The right 'nave' of the underground area abounds in the tombs of Popes and other people of note, including Nicholas V, Benedict XV, Christina of Sweden and Pius VI, whose tomb has priceless fourth-century bas-reliefs on its cover.

The left nave also contains tombs, including those of Pius II, Hadrian VI (Breakspeare — the only English Pope, died 1159), and the last of the Stuart family. In a chapel at the beginning of the nave we find a mosaic showing Christ between the Martyrs Peter and Paul: St Peter is holding three keys, and has just received the solemn commission from Jesus. The mosaic was formerly part of a single monumental complex with the sarcophagus of the Emperor Otto II.

The central nave has a niche with the statue of St Peter, enthroned — Cosmatesque work of the thirteenth or fourteenth centuries. Behind the niche a small staircase leads up into the basilica itself. The last rooms before the exit also contain collections of epigraphs, among them a fine inscription of St Damasus of the fourth century;they also have remains of carvings and some of the most typical early Christian sarcophagi, among them that of Probus.

The Vatican Caves - the tomb of John XXIII (1958-63)

Excavations beneath the basilica - the interior of a mausoleum.

EXCAVATIONS BENEATH THE VATICAN

In February 1939, the work for the siting of the tomb of Pius XI, who had expressed a desire in his will to be buried in the cave as near as possible to the Confessio, brought to light some tombs beneath the central nave of the basilica. In the past, when the basilica was being rebuilt, or when the foundations for Bernini's baldacchino were being laid, some mausoleums and sarcophagi had already been discovered, but these were the subject of very superficial examination. Pius XII was anxious that systematic excavations should take place, and on 28th June 1939, the Eve of the Feast of St Peter and St Paul, the work began. It brought to light a necropolis of the second or third century A.D., characterised by mausoleums lined up alongside a kind of street — perhaps the Via Cornelia — which were separated by *diverticula*, or narrow passageways.

Most of these are pagan: they are built with bricks, and above the entrances are plaques with the names of the owners, almost all of them of quite modest social standing. Inside, the walls are indented with small niches for placing the cinerary jars with the ashes of the deceased; they also have large arches built over the sarcophagi, or over alcoves where bodies were deposited. The interior decoration was designed so as to make the stay in this, his or her last abode, more cheerful, as far as this was possible: there are paintings of fruit, flowers, birds and other gracious ornamental features. In some cases there are also more complicated scenes, always funereal in character, like the one with a mosaic showing the Rape of Proserpine. One of the few mausoleums belonging to anybody of a certain social standing is that of Ostoria Chelidon, the daughter of Ostorius Euhodianus, consul-designate. The young girl's skeleton was found almost intact, covered with a golden veil and with a golden bracelet on her wrist.

However, there is no lack of evidence of Christianity in this necropolis. The lapidary tablet found in the tomb of the Cetenni is particularly beautiful; here a dead woman, Aemilia Gorgonia, is pictured in the act of drawing water from a well; in the epigraph beside this, her husband praises her beauty and chastity.

One of the most interesting of the mausoleums is that of the Julii, pagan in origin, as we can see from the cinerary urns which were found there, but definitely Christian by the 3rd century A.D. when it was given the splendid mosaic decoration which begins above a strip painted with imitation marble, and also covers the whole vault of the roof. Almost all the tesserae of the mosaic have fallen from the walls, but from the traces which they have left on the plaster bed, it is possible to make out the figures of Jonah, the Good Shepherd and the Divine Fisherman. The decoration on the vault is better preserved, but there is a large hole in it. At the four corners of the roof begin corresponding grape-vines which with their branches and emerald green leaves cover the vault, in the centre of which was the Christ-helios, symbol of the Resurrection, on a chariot drawn by four horses (of which only two have survived).

The greatest concern of those who explored the Vatican necropolis was to show that the altar of the Confessio rises above the tomb of Peter, as tradition asserts. And in fact, in the area below the presbytery, a little open space was found,which is known formally as 'Campo P', the shape of which seems to have been decided by the wish to preserve a reverential area around a humble earthen grave, besides which other similar sepulchres had already been built by the mid-second century A.D. Along a little road which flanked Campo P on the western side, a wall had been built, covered in plaster and painted red, (and therefore known as the Muro Rosso or Red Wall) during the 2nd century A.D. When it reaches the level of the earth tomb, this is indented to form a niche, used for a small pavilion with two thin marble columns supporting a travertine strip.

It appears to be a sort of funerary monument, probably the *tropaion* of Peter, which is mentioned by the church writer Gaius at the beginning of the 3rd century. Towards the middle of the third century a new wall was built beside the small pavilion, at right angles to the Red Wall, and soon after another was added on the other side. In the earth tomb which is marked by the pavilion, no traces of human remains were found, but a hiding-place found in the first of the two right-angle walls, (known as Wall G) did contain the bones of a male person, strongly built and of advanced years, originally shrouded in a sheet of purple and gold — all elements which seem to confirm that these really were the remains of St Peter, transferred here from the original grave on the orders of Constantine, probably to protect them from the creeping effects of water erosion. The graffiti covering the whole surface of Wall G are especially interesting; they were put there by pilgrims who had made their way to this venerated spot, and they have been studied with minute care by Prof. Margherita Guarducci, who has succeeded in interpreting their complex system of cryptographs. One of the most important is the inscription found on a piece of plaster which fell from Wall G, where we can read PETR/ENI, or "Peter is here".

A further confirmation of the existence of the tomb of the Apostle in this spot comes from the interest which Constantine showed in it; in order to have the pavilion of the Red Wall at the centre of the basilica which he began building, he had no hesitation in putting the whole of the necropolis out of service. Because it ran further up the slope, the Emperor had part of the hill cut away, and he also filled up an uneven fissure which was as much as eight metres deep, an action which was very arbitrary and against the usual Roman custom, which protected sepulchres with great rigour.

The pavilion, isolated from the rest of the necropolis, with its threshold less than 36 centimetres beneath the pavement of the basilica, rose up in the middle of the old presbytery, but it was closed inside a sort of later pavilion, open on one side only and made up of strips of porphyry and pavonazzetto marble.

Gregory the Great (590-604), in order to place the altar directly over the tomb of Peter, had the floor of the presbytery raised by one metre forty-five centimetres, and in order to give further access to the monument of Constantine he designed an original semi-ciruclar crypt, running underground beneath the outline of the apse, from the centre of which ran a passage at right-angles leading to the tomb of the Apostle. Despite the transformations suffered by the basilica over the course of the years, and its total rebuilding, every new altar of the Confessio has stood in the same place as its predecessor, so that even today the Papal altar beneath Bernini's baldacchino is exactly over the tomb of Peter. Anyone looking at the crypt decorated by Maderno can see at the centre the niche of the Palls which is just the niche of the Red Wall, decorated with a mosaic of the Saviour.

The Papal Palaces seen from Piazza San Pietro

THE PAPAL PALACES

From a passage in the Liber Pontificalis relating to the life of Pope Symmachus (498-514) we know that he built two episcopal residences near the Vatican basilica, one for himself and one for visiting bishops. These must have been very modest buiildings, to be used only on the occasion of important ceremonies in St Peter's, because the official papal residence was in the Lateran. In the course of the centuries, however, this primitive nucleus of buildings was enlarged and beautified, so that by 781 it was already adequate to house the Emperor Charlemagne.

Popes such as Eugenius III (1145-1153) and Celestine III (1191-1198) paid special attention to the Vatican Palace, and both of them undertook important restoration work. Innocent III (1198-1216), and Nicholas III (1277-1280) also enlarged it considerably.

Between 1305 and 1377, because of the transfer of the Papal Court to Avignon, the Palace was uninhabited. When they returned to Rome the Popes chose the Vatican as their official residence as the Lateran had become unusable owing to its long period of abandonment. They began a series of radical works of transformation there, and in the reign of Nicholas V (1447-1455) the existing buildings were enveloped by a square body of new buildings with the 'Courtyard of the Parrot' at the centre — the name is linked to the chapel which Nicholas had built there and decorated by Fra Angelico.

It is to Sixtus IV (1474-1484) that we owe the building of the Sistine Chapel, the work of Giovannino de' Dolci, with Frescos by Botticelli, Domenico Ghirlandaio, Cosimo Rosselli, Luca Signorelli, Pinturicchio and Perugino.

Innocent VIII (1484-1492) was responsible for the

building of the Palazzetto del Belvedere by Giacomo da Pietrasanta, while Alexander VI (1492-1503) added the 'Torre Borgia' to the Palazzetto of Nicholas V; in this tower there are two of the rooms of the sumptuous apartments of this Pope, where the decorations were painted by Pinturicchio and his students.

During the reign of Julius II (1503-1513), Bramante linked the Palazzetto del Belvedere to the other palaces by means of a corridor, and Raphael began work on the frescos of the rooms which were to take his name, and which he completed under Leo X. This latter Pope also entrusted Raphael with the completion of the loggias which form the eastern face of the Apostolic Palace. It was Julius II who ordered Michelangelo to decorate the vault of the Sistine Chapel.

Paul III (1534-1549) who committed the building of the Pauline Chapel of the Sala Regina to Antonio da Sangallo, also gave Michelangelo the order for the most amazing of all his works — the decoration of the far wall of the Sistine Chapel with the Last Judgment.

The work of embellishing, transforming and enlarging the Vatican Palaces continued in the centuries which followed, right up to the time when the great new complex begun by John XXIII (1958-1963) and continued by Paul VI (1963-1978) was completed; in this are housed the collections from the former Lateran Museum — the collection of Papal Carriages and the Missionary and Ethnographic Museum.

◀ *The Scala Regia or "Royal Staircase"*

The band of the Swiss Guards.

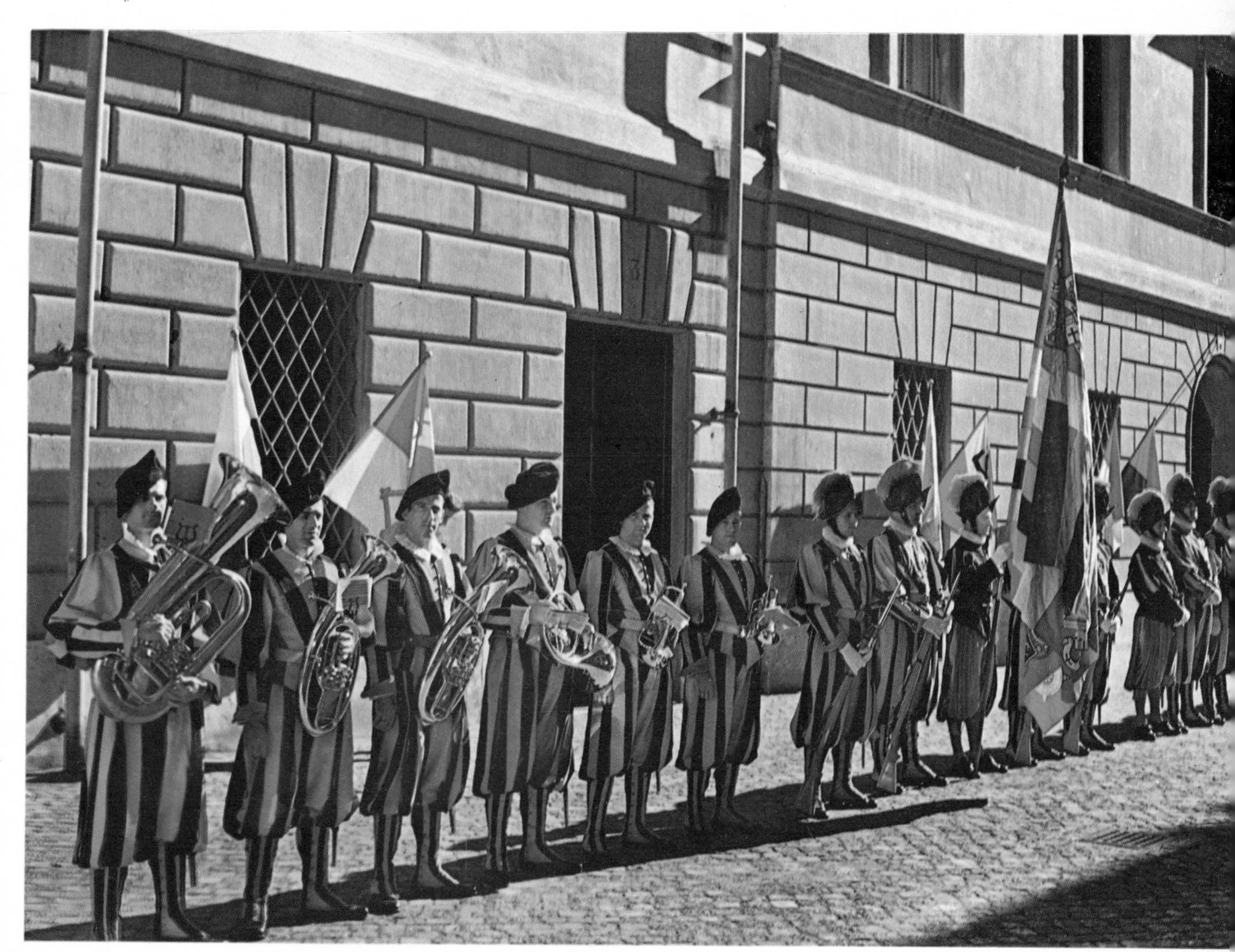

The Gallery of the Candelabras

THE VATICAN MUSEUMS

The original nucleus of the Vatican collections was made up of the ancient statuary which Julius II, with through-going Renaissance taste, had collected and set on display, mainly in the courtyard of the Palazzetto del Belvedere. This little palace was a finely balanced building put up by Innocent VIII; on the orders of Julius II, Bramante connected it with the Vatican Palace itself by means of a long corridor. Other Popes added to the collection, and Pius V (1559-1565) completed the lay-out of the Belvedere Court according to Bramante's plan. This was done by adding a second corridor, parallel to the original one and linked to it by a building at the far end in which Pirro Ligorio constructed the "Nicchione della Pigna", (the large niche containing the antique bronze pine-cone).

In the austere atmosphere of the Counter-Reformation, Pius V broke up the Vatican collections, and presented the majority of the ancient sculptures to the Roman people.

It was only in the eighteenth century that there was a revival of the collector's instinct among the Popes. Clement XII bought up Greek vases, and also formed the nucleus of the numismatic collection. Benedict XIV founded the Galleria Lapidaria and the Museo Sacra of the Library, and it is to Clement XIII that we owe the Museo Profano of the Library. Clement XIV founded a new, large museum and remodelled the Palazzetto del Belvedere, which were finished under his successor, Pius VI.

This work, entrusted to the architects Simonetti and Caporese, mainly involved the addition of an octagonal shaped portico to the Courtyard of the Belvedere, and the building of a new block of buildings which directly connected the Palazzetto with the corridor of the Library.

The collections, which were set out in the new museum (named the "Pio Clementino") by Giovan-Battista Visconti and his son Emilio Quirino, were split up during the Napoleonic period as a result of the Treaty of Tolentino in 1797, which deprived them of all their best works — fortunately restored, however, in 1816. Only the Museo Profano was to remain despoiled of the greater part of its collection.

It was Pius VII (1800-1823) who was responsible for the purchase of numerous ancient sculptures, with which he built up the Museum which is named after him, the Chiaramonte. This enlightened Pope enriched and remodelled the Galleria Lapidaria, and also caused the Braccio Nuovo to be built — a link between the two parallel corridors of the Sistine Library.

The importance of the new purchases made during the discoveries in Southern Etruria, especially at Cerveteri and Vulci in the years between 1828 and 1836 led Gregory XVI (1831-1846) to found the Museo Gregoriano Etrusco. The same Pope went on to found the Museo Egiziano with finds which were already in the possession of the Capitoline Museum and with material from Hadrian's Villa.

From that time onwards, the Vatican Museums continued to grow richer and richer in content, thanks to purchases and also to extraordinary finds which were made in the area of the Vatican City itself. Quite recently (1970) the Museums have received a notable expansion by the addition of the collections which were formerly at the Lateran, transferred here at the wish of Pope John XXIII.

THE MUSEO GREGORIANO EGIZIO

Founded in 1839 by Gregory XVI, this Museum has a display of finds which come mainly from Hadrian's Villa at Tivoli and from the foundations of the Vatican itself and the Capitoline Museum. It was first arranged by Fr. Luigi Maria Ungarelli, and the rooms were later decorated in Egyptian style following a project by De Fabris.

In the 1st ROOM, to the right of the entrance, is the

The Gregorian Egyptian Museum

reproduction of a 'serdab' - a container for the statue of the deceased and his family. Along the walls are two funeral steles, and two large statues in black granite, of the goddess with the lion's head, Sekemet, the daughter of the sun (14th century B.C.), flanked by two basalt lions from the fourth century B.C.

The 2nd ROOM has been designed as the interior of an underground chamber of a tomb from the Valley of the Kings; on the left are three great sarcophagi in the shape of the human form, made from basalt and dating fom the 16th century B.C. Behind glass there are also mummies from various periods, while on the far wall two sarcophagi in white sandstone and several canopic vases - typical funeral jars in terracotta, sandstone or alabaster, in which the intestines of the deceased were placed when they had been removed for embalming purposes. Near the right-hand wall are some wooden chests, with fine paintings of funeral ceremonies, magical formulae, and passages from the Book of the Dead.

The 3rd ROOM, which still has the decorations which were made in the last century, has Roman-Egyptian statuary from the Villa of Hadrian and the Temple of Isis in the Campus Martius (Iseo Campense). Some noteworthy works are a statue of Antinous, the youth who was divinised by Hadrian, one of the Nile, and a massive bust of Isis.

In the middle of the 4th ROOM, in a special glass case, is the magnificent wooden chest, painted inside and out, made for the mummy of the Queen Hetepheret-es.

Two statues of the goddess Sekemet stand on either side of the door leading into ROOM 5, built into the great semicircular space which faces on to the Cortile della Pigna. Here can be seen a fairly late female statue of very fine workmanship, known simply as 'La Bella'. A black granite throne displayed here belongs to a statue of Rameses II (13th century B.C.) which has unfortunately been lost. Right at the centre of the semicircle is a big statue in dark granite (approx. 1280 B.C.) of the mother of Rameses, Queen Tuia.

The sandstone head of Pharaoh Mentuhotep (11th Dynasty, 2054 - 2008 B.C.), is of great interest because of its antiquity. At the rear of the semicircle there are three statues in pink granite from the 3rd century B.C., of Ptolemy II Philadelphos, his mother Arsinoe, and a princess.

The 6th ROOM has a collection of the mummies of various sacred animals (cats, serpents and hawks), scarabs and amulets in bronze or other coloured substances. In the glass case in the centre can be seen a censer made in the shape of an arm.

In the 7th ROOM is a large collection of small statuettes.

In the centre of the 8th ROOM is the basalt statue of the 6th century B.C. showing a priest who is carrying a small temple (naophoros); similar statues from various eras are arranged along the walls.

Papyri from various epochs, together with writings in hieroglyphics and hieratical script can be seen in the 9th ROOM, while the Grassi Collection, with Egyptian objects from the Coptic period to very recent times is in the 10th and last room of the Museum.

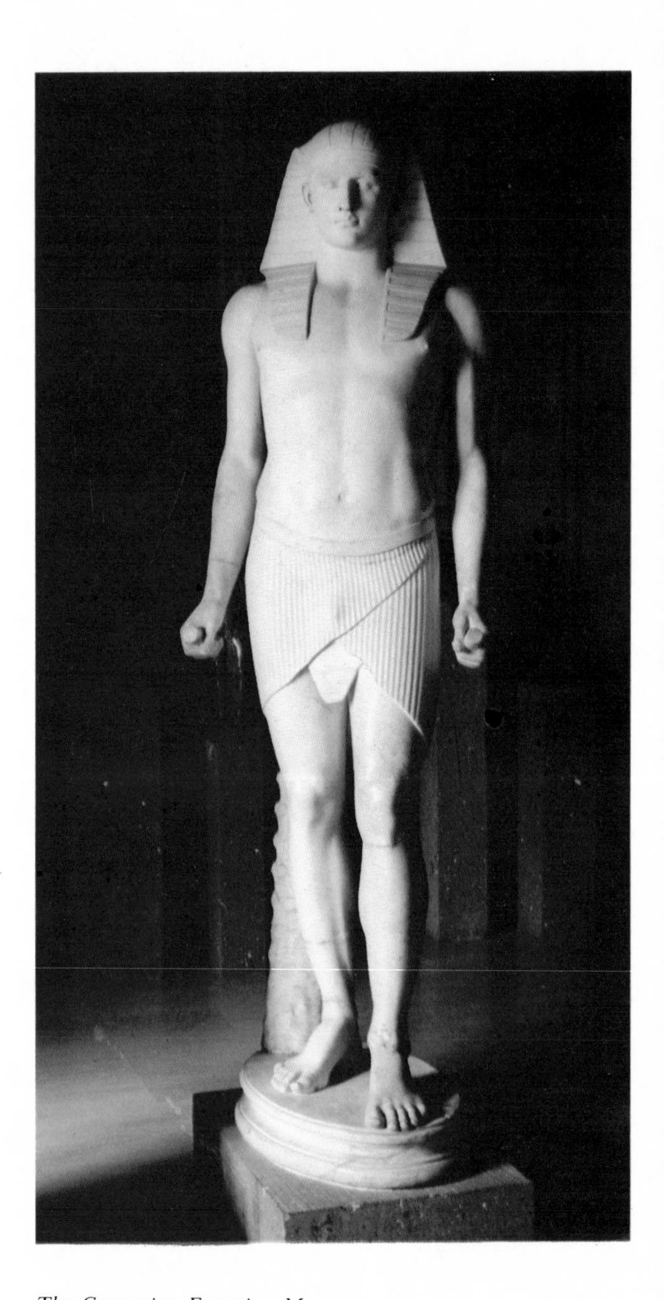

The Gregorian Egyptian Museum

The Pio Clementino Museum - The Greek Cross Room, with the sarcophagi of Helena and Constantine: at the centre of the room, a polychrome mosaic from Tusculum (3rd century)

THE PIO-CLEMENTINO MUSEUM

The Museum is housed in several rooms of the Palazzetto del Belvedere, and in the other rooms which were specially built for it by Clement XIV and Pius VI.

A visit to the Museum begins with the SALA A CROCE GRECA (Greek Cross Room) where Roman sculptures are exhibited together with mosaics from the 1st and 2nd centuries A.D., and two very beautiful sarcophagi in porphyry dating from the fourth century. Once of these is of Constantia, the daughter of Constantine and has cherubs, acanthus sprays and other reliefs from her mausoleum on the Via Nomentana (Santa Costanza). The other belongs to St Helen, the mother of Constantine, and shows barbarians being defeated by Roman knights; this comes from the mausoleum at Tor Pignattara. This latter sarcophagus, which was for a long time in the Lateran was damaged by a fire, and was extensively restored in the late eighteenth century.

There follows the SALA ROTUNDA, roofed with a dome modelled on that of the Pantheon. At the centre of the room stands a huge porophyry basin found in the Domus Aurea, while the Roman mosaic from Otricoli has been inserted into the floor. This mosaic is polychrome, with scenes representing battling centaurs and water divinities. Some of the most outstanding sculptures are a female divinity (possibly Ceres), the Barberini Juno, an Antinous-Bacchus from Palestrina, and most important of all, the famous Jove of Otricoli — a bust which reproduces the Greek original by Briasides. The enormous statue of Hercules in gilded bronze (1st century B.C. or 1st century A.D.) is also interesting.

The SALA DELLE MUSE has a vault painted by Sebastiano Conca; it consists of a central room of octagonal shape and two vestibules. In the first of these there is a statue of Lycurgus together with several

The Pio-Clementino Museum - Sarcophagus of Constantia (4th Century)

Pio-Clementino Museum - Female divinity (possibly Ceres); Roman copy of a 5th century BC Greek original.

Pio-Clementino Museum - the Room of the Animals

Pio-Clementino Museum - The Belvedere Torso, signed by Apollonius of Nestor (1st century BC)

Herms, among them that of Pericles. The general is portrayed with a calm, serene expression; a notable feature is the visor of the helmet, which Pericles has raised to his forehead, revealing his hair; it was said in fact that Pericles had a very broad cranium.

The statues of the Muses and of Apollo, together with other sculptures, are lined up along the walls of the Octagonal Room, at the centre of which, in the floor, can be seen a polychrome mosaic which comes from the Esquiline (2nd-3rd century). In the middle of this room stands the Torso del Belvedere, signed by Apollonius of Nestor, an Athenian neo-Attic sculptor who was active in Rome in the first century B.C. The powerful masculine figure, though now reduced only to a torso, excited the admiration of the artists of the Renaissance (it was discovered at the beginning of the fifteenth century) and especially of Michelangelo. Most scholars hold that the statue represents Hercules, because of the skin of the wild beast on which it is seated, but it has also been suggested that it may represent Philocthenes with a Silenus or with Polyphemus.

The large rectangular room which follows is known as the SALA DEGLI ANIMALI. One especially important feature of this room is the Roman marble reproduction of the bronze figure of Meleager by Scopas (4th century B.C.), shown with the head of the Wild Boar of Calydon, and with a dog at his feet. The most elegant group with a Triton carrying off a nymph under the eyes of two astonished pretty cherubs may be an original of the late Hellenic period, possibly by Archisilaos. On the floor of this room, and also on the walls, are Roman mosaics.

Through a door in the left-hand wall of this Room, we go on to the GALLERIA DELLE STATUE (Gallery of the Statues), the first part of which still forms part of the extensions built by Clement XIV and Pius VI, while the remaining two thirds are in the Palazzetto del Belvedere, as can be seen from the different pictorial decorations on the walls. In the gallery, a number of Roman statues are displayed, most of them copies of Greek works, and a few of Hellenistic origin, such as the bust of a Triton from Tivoli, or the sleeping figure of Ariadne. Of very great importance are the copies of the Apollo Saurochthonus, and the Resting Satyr by Praxiteles, and the Amazon in the Mattei style, a copy of one of the four statues preserved in the Temple of Artemis at Ephesus, which were made by Phydudias, Polycletus, Cresilas and Phradmon; it is thought that it portrays the Phydian type, even though the head is not consistent with this.

At the end of the Gallery on the left, beside the Sleep-

ing Ariadne and the sarcophagus showing a battle of the giants, are the two Barberini Candelabras, made of marble and of exquisite workmanship (2nd century). They came from Hadrian's Villa, and they have figures of divinities in bas-relief on the base sections.

Next comes the GALLERIA DEI BUSTI; the first room has a numerous collection of portraits of Roman Emperors, among which one of the most interesting is of Octavian as a young boy. There is also a fine head of Julius Caesar, with a very intense expression on the face. From a first century funerary monument comes the famous double half-bust of the husband and wife, Gratidia Chrite and M. Gratidius Libanus, known familiarly as Cato and Portia. In the second room are numerous busts of heros, divinities and emperors, and a head of the young Caracalla. The most famous piece in the third room is the statue of Jove known as Verospi. It shows him seated with his sceptre in his right hand and the lightning in his left.

At this point we have to turn back to the beginning of the Gallery of the Statues and move to the GABINETTO delle MASCHERE where four second century mosaic portraits have been let into the floor. They come from Hadrian's villa and three of them show stage masks, while the fourth shows a landscape. On the right hand side of this room there is a reproduction on a smaller scale of the Venus in her Bath by Diodalsas of Bithynia, portrayed bending over under a jet of water. On the far wall is the best of the numerous copies we possess of the Venus of Cnidus, the work of Praxiteles (4th century B.C.) — greatly admired by the ancients. Completely naked, while she is taking off her clothes in preparation for the bath: the right hand, the left arm and the neck are restorations, while the head, although it is an ancient work, does not belong to this statue. Near this statue there stands the marble relief showing the Three Graces. An elegant basin in antique red and a red marble satyr from the Villa of Hadrian are also to be found here.

A door from the Sala degli Animali leads into the CORTILE DEL BELVEDERE (The Belvedere Courtyard), originally a square but later transformed into an octagon by Simonetti in 1773 by adjoining an arcade whith Ionic columns. In the angles of this arcade there are the niches known as the "gabinetti" where several statues of great importance are displayed. Two Molossian hounds, from the Hellenistic period, flank the doorway, and on the right of this doorway there stands the "Gabinetto del Laocoonte" where we can see the famous work of Agesandrus of Rhodes and his two sons Athenodorus and Polydorus (approximately 2nd century B.C.). It shows, in close rhythmic harmony, and with great dramatic effect, the priest of Apollo, Laöcoon, in the act of being

The Belvedere Courtyard

Pio-Clementino Museum (Belvedere Courtyard) - The Laocoon, work signed by Agesandros, Athenodoros and Polydoros of Rhodes (approx. 2nd century B.C.) ▶

strangled, together with his two sons, by two serpents which have come without warning from the sea. The group which was found in 1506 on the Oppian Hill was incorrectly restored in the sixteenth century by Giovan Angelo Montorsoli. In 1957-58, as a result of a discovery made by the archaeologist Pollak of the right arm of Laocoon, a complete revision of the restoration was effected, and as a result of this the group now appears far more dynamic and unified than could previously have been supposed. Behind the base can be seen the right arm as reconstructed by Michelangelo, who had in fact guessed its exact position. In the portico to the left of this "gabinetto" is the plaster model of the group as it used to be in Montorsoli's restoration.

Pio-Clementino Museum - The Apoxyomenos - Roman copy of a celebrated bronze by Lysippus (c. 320 B.C.)

The "GABINETTO DEL BELVEDERE" takes its name from the world-famous statue of Apollo Belvedere, a Roman copy of an original which can be attributed to Leochares (end of the fourth century B.C.). Discovered at the end of the fifteenth century at Grottaferrata or Anzio, it was taken during the neo-classical period as the model of ideal beauty, especially by Winckelmann.

In order to replace the statues carried off by Napoleon as a result of the Treaty of Tolentino, Pius VII purchased the three statues by Canova (dating from around 1800) which stand in the GABINETTO DEL PERSEO: an elegant Perseus, inspired by the Apollo Belvedere, with the head of Medusa, and the two boxers Kreugas and Damoxenos, known to us from a passage in Pausanias' "Itinerary". In the last corner of the Courtyard is the GABINETTO DELL'ERMES, with the copy, probably dating from the time of Hadrian, of a statue of Hermes from the fourth century B.C., formerly known in error as the "Antinous of the Belvedere".

Through the door between the Gabinetto of Apollo and that of Perseus, we come into a round vestibule which leads into the SALA DELLE ISCRIZIONI, in the centre of which is the Apoxyomenos, the only reproduction which has survived of the famous masterpiece by Lysippus (c. 320 B.C.). It shows an athlete who is scraping his skin with a strigil after a race. The statue, found in Trastevere in 1849, has only undergone minor restorations: it shows clearly the innovations which were introduced by Lysippus into classical art, with a search for a new relationship between the various parts of the body, which would give the figure a new slimness and suppleness. Above all, however, there is the achievement of a three-dimensional effect, thanks to which the work is perfect from whatever angle it is viewed.

On the left wall are inscriptions in ancient Latin from the Sepulchre of the Scipioni, and a first century bas-relief showing a sacrifical procession coming from an altar. On the right is the Altar of Augustus, dedicated in the year 12 B.C. and decorated on all four sides with bas-reliefs.

At the end of the room is a small vestibule which leads into the great oval room of Bramante (beginning of the sixteenth century), and through this we can pass on to the Gregorian Etruscan Museum.

If we go instead through the Round Vestibule, we then arrive in the VESTIBOLO QUADRATO. A niche on the right hand side contains the sarcophagus of L. Cornelius Scipio Barbatus (Consul in 298 B.C.) which comes from the Sepulchre of the Scipios on the Via Appia. On the brow of this there is an inscription in Saturnine verse, containing the *elogium* of the dead man. In the window aperture there is the so-called Ara Casali, from the second or third century, decorated with bas-reliefs inspired by the legend of the origins of Rome (Mars and Venus, Romulus and Remus, and the Trojan myths).

THE CHIARAMONTE MUSEUM

The Museum takes its name from Pius VII Chiaramonte, 1800-1823, and it occupies approximately half of the long gallery built by Bramante to link the Belvedere with the Papal Palace. The lunettes in the upper part were painted according to suggestions made by Canova between 1803 and 1817. The walls of the Gallery are divided into 30 Sections by side and number.

In Section I, especially worthy of notice is the sarcophagus of Junius Enodus and his wife, Metilia Actis; this comes from Ostia and has reliefs showing the myth of Alcestis. Alcestis and his wife Admeta have the facial features of the two Roman citizens buried in the tomb.

In Section X is the characteristic funerary monument of P. Nonnius Zeto, from the 1st century A.D., made up of a squared block of marble in the upper part of which are set eight niches of conical shape for the funerary vases. At the sides of the inscription, two bas-reliefs show an ass which is turning a mill and other instruments for the making of flour.

A funerary statue of Cornutus represented as Saturn on his throne, dating from the end of the 3rd century, is placed in the twelfth Section.

In Section XVI there is a huge head of Athena, perhaps originally inserted in an acrolyth: it is a Roman copy, most likely of the type of Athena Promachos by Phydias (VI century B.C.)

In Section XIX there are some portrait busts, two of which are probably of the same Roman personage from the end of the Republican era, and another (the so-called "Scipio") of a priest of Isis, as is made clear by the shaven head and the typical scar on the forehead.

A seated statue of Tiberius is in the XXI Section, while in Section XXIII is the fragment of a bas-relief with Penelope, derived from an original of the 5th century B.C.

The XXIX Section houses two huge heads from Veio, one of Augustus and the other of Tiberius; there is also a statue of Tiberius. In Section XXXI can be found a relief showing the Three Graces, a very fine Roman copy from the end of the first century A.D., based on the original of Socrates (480-470B.C.) which was near the Propileia of the Acropolis in Athens.

Section XXV contans a fine portrait of a Roman High Priest of the first century B.C., and a fragment of a Battle of the Amazons from a neo-Attic copy in reduced proportions of the Athena Parthenos of Phydias. A statue of Hercules with his club, a replica of a Greek work of the fourth century B.C. stands in Section XXXVII and in Section XLVII there are two interesting portraits, one of the first century A.C. said to be of Silla, and the other of a woman of the Julio - Claudian family.

THE GALLERIA LAPIDARIA

Beyond the half-way point, the remainder of Bramante's long corridor is occupied by the Lapidary Gallery, a collection of epigraphs containing more than 5000 inscriptions, collected by Clement XIV (1769-74), Pius VI (1775-99) and Pius VII (1800-1823).

The pagan inscriptions are arranged on the left side of the Gallery, while the Christian ones stand on the right.

THE BRACCIO NUOVO OR NEW WING

The wide, light-filled gallery which crosses the Cortile del Belvedere a little destance from the parallel one belonging to the Biblioteca Sistina, was built during the pontificate of Pius VII by Raffaele Stern, between 1817 and 1822. The walls are punctuated by two unbroken rows of niches containing statues; between one niche and another busts are arranged on drums or corbels.

In the third niche on the right is the statue of a Silenus with the little Dionysius in his arms, a copy of the work by Lysippus (4th century B.C.)

The next niche contains the famous breast-plated statue of Augustus from Prima Porta, found in 1863 in the Villa of Livia (Augustus' mother) on the Via Flaminia, near Prima Porta. Probably a copy of a bronze original, it is the most beautiful of all the portraits of the emperor, who is shown at the age of about forty, with bare feet, and with his cuirass decorated with very fine and interesting reliefs of a historico-political kind, while he extends his right hand in the gesture of an adlocutio.

A little further on, also on the right, is a statue of Titus, wearing a toga.

Opposite the staircase are two peacocks in gilded bronze, probably from the Mausoleum of Hadrian and

MVNIF PI. IX. P.M.

subsequently placed in the portico of the early Basilica of St Peter's.

Almost at the end of the Gallery can be seen a statue of Demosthenes, a copy of the work of Polyeuctus in the Agora at Athens, which was dedicated to the great orator.

As we pass back along the Gallery in the opposite direction, we arrive at the copy of the Wounded Amazon by Cresylas (430 B.C.) restored by Thorwaldsen. After comes a statue of Juno, one of Artemis (a copy of a fourth century B.C. original) and a bust, probably of Mark Anthony, from the end of the republican era.

Opposite the semi-circle is a colossal statue of the Nile, found in 1513 in the Church of Santa Maria sopra Minerva, in the place where the Iseo Campese once stood. The river god is resting an elbow on a statue of the Sphinx, and is surrounded by sixteen cherubs, symbolising the cubits' depth which the Nile could reach during its beneficent flood period. This statue of the Roman era (first century A.C.) — but probably inspired by a Hellenistic model — was counter-balanced by that of the Tiber, found in the same place, but today kept in the Louvre in Paris.

Also along the corridor is the so-called Athena Justiniani, a good copy in Parian marble of the original bronze one attributed to Cephisodotus or Euphranor. A little way away from this stands one of the replicas of the famous Resting Satyr of Praxiteles (4th century B.C.) while at the other far end of the Gallery is the copy of the Doriphorus, the most celebrated work of Polycletus (5th century B.C.), with which the artist fixed his standard rule — the perfect relationship between the measurements of various parts of the body.

◀ *Vatican Museums - The New Wing (Braccio Nuovo) - breastplated statue of Augustus from the Villa Livia at Prima Porta.*

Vatican Museums - New Wing - The Nile (1st century)

THE CORTILE DELLA PIGNA (COURTYARD OF THE PINECONE)

On the way back to the Atrium of the Four Gates, we can turn into the Courtyard of the Pinecone. This is the northern section of the great courtyard (300 metres by 70 metres - 980 ft by 230 feet) which was planned by Bramante, closed in between the two long corridors linking the small Palace of Innocent VIII with the Papal Palaces. At the end of the sixteenth century, the cross wing of the Biblioteca Sistina was added to divide the courtyard into two halves; after the work done by Raffaele Stern (1817-1822) it was further divided into three: the Cortile della Pigna, the Cortile of the Biblioteca, and that of the Belvedere.

The Courtyard of the Pinecone owes its name to a huge Roman pinecone which stands before a niche built by Pirro Ligorio in 1560, at the far end of the courtyard. The cone, which stands on a splendid carved capital of the third century, most probably comes from the Iseo Campense, where it formed part of the decoration of a fountain; it was subsequently transferred to the Atrium of the primitive Basilica of St Peter's . On either side of the cone are two bronze peacocks, from the Mausoleum of Hadrian.

Beneath the niche stood the base of the commemorative column of Antoninus Pius (138-161), on the front of which is represented the apotheosis of the Emperor and his wife Faustina. This has now been rehoused in the Cortile delle Corazze.

The Courtyard of the Pine-cone - Niche of Pirro Ligorio, and the Pine-cone itself

THE SALA DELLA BIGA (THE ROOM OF THE CHARIOT)

From a staircase near the Greek Cross Room, we go up to the large round room with a domed roof built by Camporesi during the reign of Pius VI (1775-1799). It takes its name from the imposing chariot in the middle of the room, built in 1788 by F.A. Franzoni by using ancient fragments (the right-hand horse and the body of the chariot) probably coming from a Roman votive chariot susequently used as an episcopal throne in the Church of St Mark.

Along the walls of this room interesting pieces of sculpture have been arranged, among which (at the right of the entrance) is a bearded statue of Dionysius, a first century copy of a fourth century (B.C.) Greek original. Also from the first century is the toga'd statue of an elderly Roman.

A Discobolus who is measuring out the ground is also worth noting; he is preparing to throw his discus; the original of this statue is attributed to Naucides, the son of Polycletus (5th century B.C.).

The most important work in the room, however, is the marble copy (dating from Hadrian's reign) of the very famous Discobolus of Myron (fifth century B.C.), which portrays a young athlete at the moment when he is about to hurl his discus.

Vatican Museum - Room of the Chariot - the great chariot built by F.A. Franzoni (1788) out of various ancient fragments.

THE MUSEO GREGORIANO ETRUSCO

The Etruscan Museum was founded by Gregory XVI in 1837. It mainly houses finds from Southern Etruria, and it also possesses an important collection of Greek and Italiot vases, as well as a collection of Roman antiquities.

The *1st ROOM*, also known as the *ROOM OF THE SARCOPHAGI*, has two lions dating from the 6th century B.C., from Vulci, a city where such statues were very frequently placed on guard at the entrance to the tombs. In the centre of the room there are some sarcophagi, one of which has reliefs on the chest showing scenes from the myth of Orestes, Clytemnestra and Oedipus, and on the cover the figure of the person buried within, laid out in the sleep of death, while another, from the Great Tomb of Tuscania (2nd century B.C.) is decorated with the massacre of the Niobedes on the long side, and with Achilles with the corpse of Hector and a battle of the centaurs on the short sides. A sarcophagus of particular interest is the one known as 'The Magistrate's', also from Tuscania. On the front of this is shown the procession which accompanies the dead man on his last voyage; he is shown laid out on a chariot with two lictors walking ahead. Another sarcophagus shows a funeral procession on the front of the chest, and the deceased laid out on the lid. The relief on this sarcophagus still has some of its original colouring.

The *2nd ROOM*, with frescos by Federico Barocci and Taddeo Zuccari (1563), contains the sumptuous equipment from the Regolini-Galassi Tomb, found untouched in 1836 at Cerveteri, in the necropolis of Sorbo. The tumulus-style tomb, from the period when Eastern influences predominated (about 650 B.C.), yielded up a very richly decorated piece of funerary furniture, with marvellous gilding work, which shows what skill the Etruscan artists possessed even in that remote age.

Characteristic of this 'eastern' period are the large bronze basins, found in the tomb together with a cart, the remains of a chariot, a tripod, vases and bucchero figures.

The 3rd ROOM contains the bronzes, with some funerary furnishings, and objects of everyday use, as well as two statuettes of seated children, both with a 'bulla' round their necks. There are dedicatory inscriptions written on their bodies. One of the two children is shown playing with a bird.

In the centre of the room is the most interesting piece in the Museum — a great bronze statue of the 4th century BC, found in 1835 near Todi, showing a warrior dressed in a short tunic and a cuirass — possibly the God Mars (the statue is certainly known as the 'Mars of Todi'). The work, which shows clear classical influence, surely comes from an Etruscan workshop. It is characterised by a gentle plasticity, and reveals the hand of a quite expert artist, even if not of the highest class. The helmet, the lance and the eye-balls are missing; they must have been in a different material from bronze. On the cuirass, an inscription in the Umbrian tongue is carved, and it shows the statue to have been a votive gift of Ahal Trutitis.

In the same room, in glass cases, there are mirrors, cysts, candelabras, paterae and other small bronze objects. Many mirrors were found in the tombs of Etruria; they have one side polished to act as a mirror, while the other side is almost invariably decorated with engravings or reliefs, with scenes taken from Greek mythology. A mirror from Vulci is especially noteworthy; it can be dated to around 470 BC., and it has reliefs of Eos (The Dawn) who is carrying off Kephalos. Also from Vulci is

Vatican Museum: Room of the Chariot - Roman copy of the Discobolus of Myron (5th century BC)

Gregorian Etruscan Museum - Golden Pectoral from the Regolini - Galassi Tomb at Cerveteri (7th century BC)

a beautiful oval cyst (a sort of receptacle containing objects for personal care) in bronze, from the 3rd or 2nd centuries BC., decorated in embossed work showing a battle of the Amazons. The handle of the cyst is made up of two figurines of a satyr and a nymph astride swans.

In the first division of the FOURTH ROOM is exhibited material from the Villanova period, especially the two-headed vases and brooches in the shape of leeches, mainly from Vulci. In the second area are ceramics in paste and bucchero from the 7th-6th centuries B.C., while the third area has funerary urns in alabaster, marble and travertine, mainly from Volterra, Chiusi and Perugia. The chests are decorated with reliefs, chiefly inspired by the Theban myth or the Trojan legends, while the lids all have figures of the deceased, showing marked facial differences. One particularly interesting urn is the alabaster one, probably from Volterra, in a good state of preservation, with a married couple dining as its cover decoration. On the chest of this urn the race between Pelops and Enomaos is represented in dramatic style, in the presence of demons which are purely Etruscan in character.

Next comes the 5th, or GUGLIELMI, ROOM, where the collection of that name is displayed; it was donated in 1937 by the Marquis Benedetto Guglielmi to Pius XI. The collection includes painted ceramics, both Greek and Etruscan, bronzes, and gold and bucchero work (characteristic black polished Etruscan work), from the necropolis of Vulci.

In the 6th ROOM (known as 'Dei PREZIOSI') there is a rich collection of jewellery, mainly found at Vulci, which shows the high level of perfection reached by the Etruscans in metalwork, especially in the special techniques of granulation and filigree. In Case A there is a pair of golden ear-rings with rock-crystals and pietradura, from the end of the 6th century B.C., and some gold and silver-gilt rings which are either embossed or engraved. Case B contains objects made from amber, among them a horse's head from the end of the 5th century B.C. and a head of Silenus with a goatskin on his shoulder (round 500 B.C.); also rings with their settings in the shape of similar objects from Egypt. In case C are numerous *bullae*, two of which have Zeus and Athena in a four wheeled chariot. A third one, made of gold like the others, shows Aphrodite between Adonis and Eros (4th century B.C.). Cases E and F contain funerary diadems made out of very fine gold plates. (4th - 2nd centuries B.C.).

The 7th ROOM has, in chronological order, terracottas, found in Etruria and Latium, beginning with the characteristic Villanovan two-headed cinerary urns from Tarquinia and Vulci (9th - 8th centuries B.C.). The tomb furnishings of the Iron Age in the Latium shown in Case E were found in the course of excavations carried out in 1816-17 between Marino and Castelgandolfo. In Case F there is an interesting acroterium in the form of a winged horse, 5th century B.C., found at Cerveteri. From Tuscania comes the funerary monument with the dying Adonis, abandoned on a *Kliné* (couch). This richly decorated monument can be seen in Case M (2nd or 1st century B.C.).

The 8th ROOM is divided into three, and here the Antiquarium Romanum can be found. Together with objects of common use, it has freizes, reliefs and sculptures, also some ceramic cups from Arezzo (1st century B.C. to 1st century A.D.) with very fine decoration, some Roman glass, and the head of an Emperor crowned with laurel (3rd century).

The second division of the ANTIQUARIUM ROMANUM leads into the 9th ROOM of the Museum, where the Falcioni Collection of Etruscan and Roman objects is displayed.

Gregorian Etruscan Museum - The Mars of Todi

The three subsequent rooms, known as the SALE DEGLI ORIGINALI GRECI, have a collection of ancient Greek sculptures — most of them fragmentary. In the 1st room there is an Attic bas-relief with a funeral banquet, showing Hades and Persephone, and a 5th century B.C. relief showing horsemen.

In the centre of the second Room there is a fragment of the head of a horse which comes from the western pediment of the Parthenon, in which Phydias (5th cent. B.C.) portrayed the contest between Athena and Poseidon for dominion over Attica. Also from the Parthenon comes a bearded head belonging to a metope from the south side (447-440 B.C.) and a child's head with a basket, which formed part of the frieze on the northern side of the Temple (approx. 440 B.C.). To the left of the entrance can be found one of the most beautiful Greek reliefs which has come down to us; the Stele of Palestrita, dating from the mid fifth century B.C. This is a funerary stele about six feet high, showing a young athlete to whom a serving-boy is handing the *ariballos* with the oil. The incisive lines and concern for detail in this work, such as the curls of the athlete's hair, the veins, the musculature, etc., bring it close to the sculpture of Myron in quality.

Also very interesting is a large head of a female divinity, possibly Athena (44 cm high), which must have been part of an acrolite — one of those statues which had only the exposed parts carved in marble; the hands, face and feet. The two holes at the temples were for the fixing of a head-dress in bronze — probably a helmet — while the irises and pupils of the eyes, now missing, would have been in pietradura. It is believed that the work was produced around the mid fifth century B.C. in Sicily or Magna Grecia.

In the third Room on the left is an Attic votive bas-relief of the 4th century B.C. with Asclepius, Hygea and Asclepius' children.

ROOMS IX and X of the Etruscan Museum have the VASE COLLECTION, mostly from Southern Etruria, especially Vulci. It should be borne in mind that very many of the Greek ceramics which have come down to us were in fact found in Etruscan tombs, where they constituted delicate and often very expensive tomb-furnishings.

In the SALA ASTARITA there is a large late Corinthian crater with Ulysses and Menelaus demanding the return of Helen (560 B.C.), which is part of the collection given to Paul VI by M. Astarita in 1967.

In the ROOM situated in the great semi-circle of the Courtyard of the Pine-Cone, there can be seen an Attic wine-jug with black figures, by the painter of Amasis (around 525 B.C.) (Case A); an Attic cup with red figures by the painter of Brygos (around 480 B.C.) Case H), showing Hermes hiding in the cradle after the theft of Apollo's herd, and an Attic amphora with black figures signed by the famous potter and painter, Exekias (Case F). This is one of the masterpieces of Attic ceramic work; Achilles and Ajax are portrayed in a harmonious, unified composition as they play at dice. It is interesting to see with what skill the details have been captured, thanks to the use of the engraver's bulin.

Gregorian Etruscan Museum - Vase

The Vatican Library - The Sistine Room

THE VATICAN LIBRARY

The Vatican Library was founded on 15th June 1475 by Sixtus IV; it owed its institution mainly to the 1500 manuscripts which had been collected by Nicholas V (1447 to 1555)

In 1481 Sixtus IV had the library placed on the ground floor of the palace of Nicholas V, and employed Melozzo da Forlì to decorate it, aided by Antoniazzo Romano and Domenico and Davide Ghirlandaio. In the years which followed, the Popes constantly increased the collection with manuscripts and printed volumes, and eventually — between 1587 and 1589 — Sixtus V got Domenico Fontana to put up a new building to house the Library, which was given the name 'Sala Sistina'. It cut the great Belvedere Courtyard into two sections.

From the Atrium of the Four Gates we come into the Secular Museum (Museo Profano) of the Library, and thence into the Galleria Clementina, added to the Library by Clement XII in 1732, and painted with frescos by Domenico de Angelis in 1818, showing scenes from the life of Pius VII. The next room is the Sala Alessandrina, which was built under Alexander VII (in 1690); here the frescos showing the life of Pius VI are also by Domenico de Angelis. After the two rooms known as the Sale Paoline, built under Paul V (1605-1621) and decorated by G.B. Ricci with episodes in the life of this Pope (dating from 1620) the great Sala Sistina opens on the left. It is divided into two aisles, by imposing pillars which support a cross-vault. The rich decoration was carried out by a large group of artists under the direction of Giovanni Guerra (1540-1618) and Cesare Nebbia (1536-1614). They are very important from the documentary standpoint, as they show views of contemporary Rome, painted in the lunettes of the windows and at the base of the arcades. In the many showcases of the Sala some of the most important volumes and manuscripts of the Library are displayed.

We then go back to the corridor, and pass through

two rooms which bear the name of Sixtus V, leading to the Gallery of Urban VIII, which was decorated by Giovan Paolo Schor and Giovanni Angeloni. From here we go on to the Museo Sacro, begun in 1756 by Benedict XIV, and reserved for ancient christian finds, among which is a fourth century disc with the most ancient known portrait of Saints Peter and Paul, and a Byzantine mosaic from the twelfth or thirteenth century, showing St. Theodore.

Gilded glass from the third and fourth century is displayed in the next room, known as the Sala dei Papyri. From here we go on to the Sala degli Indirizzi, where some minor objets d'art are displayed.

On the right is the Sala delle Nozze Aldobrandine, on the walls of which are ancient paintings, among them the 'Marriage of the Aldobrandini' from which the room takes its name - a celebrated fresco found in the Esquiline in 1605, probably showing the preparations for the marriage of Alexander the Great and Roxana.

The Sala degli Indirizzi leads (at the far end) to the Chapel of St. Pius V (1566-1572), with frescos by Jacopo Zucchi, based on drawings by Vasari. In a glass case are some objects from the Treasury of the Sancta Sanctorum in the Lateran.

THE GALLERY OF THE CANDELABRAS

The Gallery of the Candelabras occupies less than one third of the long corridor above that of the Library. Originally it was conceived as a separate loggia, but it was closed in during the reign of Pius VI (1775-1799), by the architects Simonetti and Camporesi. The ceiling was painted between 1883 and 1887 by Domenico Torri and Ludwig Seitz.

The Gallery is divided into arcades in six sections, where apart from the extremely beautiful candelabras in marble, dating from the 2nd century A.D., there are also sculptures from the Roman Imperial Era and copies of Greek statues, such as Ganymede carried off by the Eagle, by Leochares, or the personification of the City of Antioch by Eutychides.

Of special interest are an Ephesian Diana, symbol of fruitfulness, found at Tivoli in the Villa Adriana; and two sarcophagi, one with scenes from the myth of Orestes and the other with the destruction of the Niobedes, both dating from the second century A.D. There are also ten fragments of Roman frescos and a mosaic with a still-life (2nd century A.D.) found in 1817 in a villa at Tor Marancia.

THE GALLERY OF THE ARRASES

From the Gallery of the Candelabras we pass on to that of the Arrases, where there were ten Arras tapestries by Raphael, known as the 'Scuola Vecchia'; subsequently these were transferred to the Vatican Picture Gallery. At present on the walls opposite the windows there are ten big Flemish arrases, known as 'The New School', made at Brussels by Pieter Van Aelst, on the basis of cartoons by the school of Raphael. They show scenes from the life of Christ (The Adoration of the Shepherds, the Adoration of the Magi, the Presentation in the Temple, Three Episodes from the Massacre of the Innocents, the Resurrection, Jesus appearing to Mary Magdalene, the Supper at Emmaus, and the Ascension).

On the opposite side, there are six seventeenth century arrases with events from the life of Urban VIII, and with the Countess Matilda giving her possessions to the Holy See: these are by the Roman School of the Barberini.

THE GALLERY OF THE GEOGRAPHICAL MAPS

This is a very long gallery (120 metres in all) frescoed with the Geographical Maps of Italy by Antonio Danti, based on the findings of his brother, Fr. Ignazio Danti of Perugia (1536-86) a Dominican with a very high reputation as a mathematician and cosmographer. This work, carried out between 1580 and 1583, represents the various regions of Italy, the islands of Sicily, Corsica and Sardinia, the property of the Holy See at Avignon, and also Corfù and Malta; all done with considerable accuracy in forty frames along the walls. There are also plans and views of cities; in some of the geographical maps the sites of battles are also shown, and in the case of the battle of Lepanto, which is illustrated in all its details, the painting is a historical document of great importance.

The ceiling was richly decorated by Cesare Nebbia and other artists, under the direction of Gerolamo Muziano of Brescia (1528-1590) showing episodes in the lives of some of the saints.

THE RAPHAEL STANZAS

The Rooms painted by Raphael, known as the *Stanze* are almost all in the building constructed under Nicholas V (1447-55), on the ground floor of which Sixtus IV (1471-84) had sited the Apostolic Library. Alexander VI (1492-1503) lived there on the first floor (the Borgia Apartment) and he had this sumptuously decorated by Perugino and his students. Julius II, who refused contemptuously to live in the same place as his predecessor "of most evil and villainous memory", called on some of the greatest painters of the time, such as Pinturicchio, Baldassarre Puruzzi, Sodoma and Lorenzo Lotto, to complete the decorations which had already been begun by Piero della Francesca, Luca Signorelli and others, on the second floor of the building, to which he wanted to transfer his own residence.

At the end of 1508, however, Julius, who had a particular flair for spotting great artistic talent, got to know a young artist from Urbino, Raffaello Sanzio, and decided to entrust the frescos of the papal apartment to him, even though he was then barely twenty five years old. For this purpose he removed the paintings formerly done by the other artists, despite the fact that they themselves were of no mean reputation.

In 1509 Raphael began the decoration of the four rooms, of which the first three have cross-vaulted ceilings while the fourth was provided with a false ceiling in the sixteenth century since (as it was part of the original mediaeval residence of the Popes) it formerly had a flat ceiling.

The young artist from Urbino began with the frescos in the second Stanza, which is known as the 'Segnatura' (Signature). In 1511 he went on to undertake those in the third room, known as that of 'Heliodorus'; the first Stanza, that of the 'Fire in the Borgo' was begun in 1514. The painting of the last Stanza, that of 'Constantine' was commissioned in 1517, but is was almost entirely executed by his pupils under Pope Clement VII, after the death of the artist himself, which took place in 1520.

The decoration of the *Stanza dell'Incendio di Borgo* (1514-17) takes as its theme the miraculous protection God accords to His Church, while at the same time it

◀ *The Gallery of the Arrases - Arras with the Resurrection of Our Lord, from a drawing by the school of Raphael*

◀ *The Gallery of the Geographical Maps*

Raphael Stanzas - The Fire in the Borgo

Raphael Stanzas - Detail of the Dispute of the Sacrament

Raphael Stanzas - The School of Athens. At the centre of the composition Plato and Aristotle can be seen. At the same level on the left, Socrates is debating with Alexander and Alcibiades (in armour). In the left foreground are Epicurus crowned with vine-leaves and Pythagoras who is expounding to his pupils. The person with the turban standing behind him may be Averroes. A little way away, sitting alone and separated from the others is the meditative figure of Heraclitus, in whom Raphael portrayed Michelangelo. The cynic Diogenes is shown lying full length on the steps. In the group in the right foreground we can make out Euclid (a portrait of Bramante), bending over a board, Zoroastro, with the celestial sphere in his hand, and Ptolemy, crowned and a little behind, with a globe in his hand. Beside Euclid in the far corner on the right are portraits of Sodoma, dressed in white, and Raphael himself with the long hair and black cap.

pays homage to the political position of the then Pope, Leo X (1513-1521), by means of various incidents in the lives of his illustrious predecessors with the same name — Leo III and Leo IV, who are always shown with the face of Leo X. Giulio Romano, Penni and Perin del Vega all took part in completing the frescos in this room, 'The Oath of Leo III', 'The Crowning of Charlemagne', and "The victory of Leo IV over the Saracens'. In the fresco 'The Fire in the Borgo', however, Raphael's own hand is clearly recognisable, influenced by Michelangelo's style in the powerful nudes with their heavy musculature. The ceiling of this room still has the paintings executed by Perugino in 1508.

The *Stanza della Segnatura* was originally the study and library of Julius II, and thus was decorated with frescos concerning the three fundamental principles of neo-Platonic philosophy — transmitted by way of the thought of St. Thomas Aquinas: Truth, the outcome of the union between Faith and Philosophy, Beauty derived from Poetry, and finally Well-being, obtained by Justice.

The first fresco in order of time was the one which takes Faith as its theme — or more properly Theology. The fresco is wrongly known as 'The Dispute of the Sacrament', but it actuallly shows the triumph of Religion, with the Church Triumphant adoring the Trinity in heaven, and the Church Militant on earth adoring the Eucharistic Mystery.

Philosophy is symbolised by 'The School of Athens', where the great philosophers and scientists of the past move about and debate with each other in the open area of a basilica designed by Bramante. At the centre of the composition are Plato and Aristotele considered to be the principal philosophers of the ancient world.

For Poetry, Raphael has given us 'Parnassos' — Apollo with his lyre is shown on the mythical mountain, surrounded by Muses and by the major poets, from Homer to Dante.

When it came to Justice, the painter chose two episodes to represent it: 'Gregory the Great consigning the Decretals' (representing Ecclesistical Law) and 'Justinian consigning the Pandette' (representing Civil Law). Above the frescos is a lunette with the allegories of Prudence and Temperance, on the vaulted ceiling of the room, in large medallions, are the allegories of Theology, Justice, Philosophy and Poetry, alternating with four rectangular scenes of 'Original Sin', 'The Judgment of Solomon', 'Astronomy' and 'Apollo and Marsyas' — all of them by Raphael.

The third room, the 'Stanza di Eliodoro' (1511-1514), has the principal theme of the triumph of the Papacy, while on the ceiling there are biblical scenes painted by Guglielmo da Marcillat, on the basis of designs by Raphael.

The fresco on the entrance wall shows 'Leo I stopping the invasion of Attila'; instead of being set in Lombardy (where the event took place) it is placed near Rome, and the background is formed by ruined acqueducts and the Colosseum, together with a basilica. Leo I has, once more, the face of Leo X.

On the right-hand wall is the 'Mass of Bolsena', portraying the miracle which took place in 1263 confirming the presence of Christ in the Eucharist. In this fresco Raphael revealed an extraordinary ability to create chromatic effects and contrasts, and to convey the sense of spirituality through brilliant use of light effects. Julius II is portrayed kneeling before the altar.

On the opposite wall to that of 'Leo I and Attila' is 'The Expulsion of Heliodorus from the Temple', probably an allusion to the policy of Julius II aimed at expelling foreigners from Papal territory. Of all the works of Raphael (here aided by Giulio Romano and Giovanni da Udine) this is the one with the most movement and the most dramatic effects, augmented by a light which violently permeates the whole scene.

On the left-hand wall is 'The Liberation of St Peter', to which Giulio Romano also contributed. The scene is taking place at night, and the light which shines from the evanescent figure of the angel is the real main actor in the drama, contrasting with the black bars of the prison, the pale light of the moon, and the more vivid light of the oil-lamps.

The decoration of the *Stanza di Costantino* was carried out almost entirely after Raphael's death, and has many of the marks of the rhetorical style of his pupils, who never succeded in attaining the classical vision and origi-

TIMEO
ETIC
A.

nality of their Master. The theme uniting these four frescos is the victory of Christianity over Paganism.

On the wall opposite the entrance is 'The Apparition of the Cross to Constantine' by Giulio Romano; on the wall opposite the windows 'The Battle of Constantine at Ponte Milvio', by Giulio Romano (for which Raphael had left some drawings, however); on the entrance wall is 'The Baptism of Constantine' by Francesco Penni, and on the window wall 'The Donation of Constantine' by Francesco Penni and Giulio Romano.

The beamed ceiling of this room was substituted by a false vault during the reign of Pius IV (1559-65), and this was painted by Tommaso Laureti and other artists around 1585.

Raphael Stanzas - Detail from the School of Athens: Plato (probably a portrait of Leonardo da Vinci)

Raphael Stanzas - Detail from the fresco of the 'Expulsion of Heliodorus from the Temple'.

Chapel of Nicholas V - Beato Angelico: St. Lawrence before the Judgment Seat of the Emperor Decius. At the right, behind the bars of a window, can be seen the conversion of St. Hippolytus.

THE CHAPEL OF NICHOLAS V

The Chapel is in one of the most ancient parts of the Vatican Palaces; the part which dates back to the first years of the thirteenth century. It takes its present name from Pope Nicholas V (1447-1455), who caused the frescos to be painted here by Fra' Giovanni da Fiesole, known as Beato Angelico (1400- 1455); they tell the life-story of the martyrs St Stephen and St Lawrence.

The paintings, rich in poetic inspiration, are in two ranks one above the other, divided by a freize with laurel leaves and flowers. In the lower part, are episodes in the life of St Lawrence, while in the upper part contained in large roundels, are scenes from the life of St Stephen.

The pilaster strips in the corners of the Chapel are decorated whith Gothic niches, in which there are portraits of the Doctors of the Church; St Jerome, St Augustine, St Thomas Aquinas, St Ambrose, St John Chrysostom, St Leo the Great, St Athanasius, and Pope St Gregory.

On each of the four groins of the vault there are figures of the Evangelists on clouds.

RAPHAEL'S LOGGIAS

The Loggias built by Raphael are on the second floor of the ancient building of Nicholas III (1277-1280), which Julius II had begun to close up with two orders of arcades, one above the other, following a plan by Bramante. The work was to be continued under Leo X, and on the death of Bramante in 1514, it was handed over to Raphael. He waited until 1518 to complete the architectural and decorative work on the loggias of the upper floor, formed by a series of thirteen arches, with pavilion vaulting, the first twelve of which are painted with 48 small scenes from the Old Testament (four for each archway) while the last has episodes from the New Testament.

The walls and the pilasters are covered with rich stucco decoration and grotesques, in bright and varied colours, and with a deep formal and spiritual adherence to the classical style; however they were unfortunately damaged by the ravages of time and the atmosphere. (The loggia was only cased in with windows around the middle of the nineteenth century, during the pontificate of Pius IX). The work was actually carried out by Giovanni da Udine and Perin del Vaga, who made use of a close and impassioned study of Roman antiquity. Giovanni da Udine, in particular, who did the stucco work, must have studied the reliefs found in the excavation of the Domus Aurea with very close attention, and he may even have used casts. The name 'grotesque' is derived from 'grotte', the name which was then given to excavations, and it refers to the imitation of Roman wall-decoration, which from that time onward formed part of the decorative vocabulary of Rome and thence of the whole of Europe.

The subjects are of the most varied kind, such as flowers, real and mythical animals, fruit, tiny mythological scenes and incidents in the history of those days.

In one of the stuccos Raphael's workshop is shown, while in a small medallion on the third pilaster towards the courtyard, there is a portrait of Michelangelo. Leo X is featured in one of the stuccos of the left-hand splays of the fourth arch, pictured as he walks in this very loggia and blesses a prelate who is kneeling before him. There are also representations of famous sculptures, such as the head of the Apollo Belvedere or Donatello's St. George.

Turning to the frescos on the ceiling, Raphael very probably designed the sketches for the scenes, apart from the overall design of the loggias themselves, and then they were completed by his disciples, Francesco Penni, Giulio Romano, Giovanni da Udine, Perin del Vaga, aided by Pellegrino da Modena, Vincenzo da San Gimignano and Tommaso Vincidor da Bologna, who painted the frescos of the thirteenth arch. In the scene of Moses Saved from the Waters in the eighth archway, we may suppose that Raphael himself had a hand.

The floor was made of polychrome tiles made in Florence in the Della Robbia workshop. It was removed in 1869 because it was too worn, but some of the tiles can still be seen in the Church of San Silvestro al Quirinale, in the Chapel of Fra' Mariano Fetti.

The Raphael Loggias

Borgia Apartment - Room of the Liberal Arts - Astronomy, shown as a woman with an armillary sphere in her hand, with cherubs on either side holding the smbols of the sun and moon (Pinturicchio and his helpers)

THE BORGIA APARTMENT

The Apartment takes its name from Pope Alexander VI (1492 to 1503), Rodrigo Borgia, who lived and died here. It is made up essentially of six rooms, of which the first two are in the tower which Alexander VI also caused to be built to complete the defences of his home. The three following rooms, on the other hand, were sited in the fifteenth century palace of Nicholas V, beneath the rooms which came to be known as the Raphael Stanze, while the last, the largest of all, is part of the mediaeval residence of the Popes, like the Constantine Room which lies above it.

The Apartment was superbly decorated with frescos between 1492 and 1495, by Bernardino di Betto, known to history as "Pinturicchio", and his pupils (Benedetto Bonfigli, Piero d'Andrea and Antonio da Viterbo, known as "Il Pastura", and others).

The first room is known as the "SALA DELLE SIBILLE", and it has rather austere decorations in twelve lunettes with one prophet and one apostle; each apostle is holding in his hand a scroll with a sentence from the Apostles' Creed or Credo, which is echoed in the words on the scrolls carried in the hands of each of the prophets.

The SALA DELLE ARTI LIBERALI must have been intended as Alexander's study, and for that reason the lunettes were painted (mainly by Pastura) with the Arts of the Trivium (Grammar, Dialectics, Rhetoric) and the Quadrivium (Geometry, Arithmetic, Music and Astronomy), portrayed as exquisite Madonnas of the Umbrian Renaissance tradition. The two cross vaults are decorated with grotesques, while the arch which separates them was painted round the year 1520 with allegorical scenes illustrating the theme of Justice. The chimney in inlaid marble is particularly fine, and is probably the work of Simone Mosca, based on a design by Sansovino (XVI century).

In the SALA DEI SANTI, the pictorial decorations were not only planned by Pinturicchio but for the most part carried out by him as well, as can be seen from the elegance of the design, the decorative quality, and the deep colour-sense and lively imagination. The two cross vaults of the room are decorated with friezes and stuccos with the myths of Isis, Osiris and the bull Apis (an allusion to the bull on the Borgia coat of arms), while in the lunettes are scenes from the lives of some of the saints.

In the big lunette opposite the window is one of Pinturicchio's masterpieces, the Dispute of St. Catherine of Alexandria with the Doctors of the Church before the Emperor Maximianus. The scene is set in an idyllic landscape, rich in small details, at the centre of which stands an arch similar to that of Constantine, partly depicted in relief, by the use of gilded stucco, and surmounted by the Borgia Tower. The Emperor, seated on a sumptuous throne, is listening to the Saint, a slender, graceful figure, who is defending the Christian faith. The two are surrounded by a small crowd, in which there are many portraits of contemporary people, though it is hard to identify them with any degree of certainty.

According to some authorities, the man with the coat of many colours and the long drooping moustaches to the right of the Emperor is Prince Djem, a hostage at the Papal Court and friend of the Duke of Valentino (Cesare Borgia). Others say that the figure represents Andreas Paleologos. Beside him can be seen Antonio di Sangallo the Elder, shown with a set-square in his hand, and Pinturicchio himself beside him.

In the smaller lunette on the right is shown The Visit of St. Anthony the Abbot to Saint Paul the Hermit, in which Pinturicchio may have been assisted by Pastura.

Borgia Apartment - Room of the Liberal Arts - Arithmetic, with the compass and the Pythagorean tables in her hand. The old man in the centre foreground is possibly Pythagoras. (Pinturicchio and helpers)

The scene is set in the desert of Egyptian Thebes. Three devils with female attributes who are advancing from the left-hand side of the picture represent temptation.

The fresco of the Visitation, in the next lunette, painted with all the fresh grace of a miniature, is clearly entirely from the hand of the master. The meeting between the Virgin and Saint Elizabeth takes place beneath a portico which is partly done in relief work, illuminated by gold stucco.

In the Martyrdom of St. Sebastian, which Pinturicchio depicted as taking place on the Palatine, with the Colosseum in the background, a naif interest in archaeology is revealed in the drums of the columns and capitals which are scattered all over the scene. In the other two lunettes, showing Susanna and the Elders and The Legend of St. Barbara there is a careful search for decorative effects.

On the big archway which divides the room in two, the panels illustrate the story of Argo of the hundred eyes and Io, who because she was loved by Jove was

Borgia Apartment - far wall of the Room of the Mysteries. In the first lunette is the Annunciation, which has a triumphal archway adorned with two towers (a reference to the coat of arms of the Borgias) in the background. In the second lunette can be seen the Nativity of our Lord, attributed to Bartolomeo di Giovanni.

transformed into a cow by jealous Juno.

Above the exit door Pinturicchio painted, inside a round frame in gold stucco, a gentle Madonna and Child, which some experts say is a portrait of Giulia Farnese.

In the SALA DEI MISTERI Pinturicchio and his pupils depicted the principal Mysteries of the life of Jesus and of the Virgin. The cycle begins with the lunette to the right of the far wall, the Annunciation, after which follows the Birth of Jesus, characterised by a gentle and fabulous landscape like that of the Adoration of the Magi, which comes next.

In the scene of the Resurrection we can see one of Pinturicchio's great masterpieces, a portrait of Alexander VI who is shown kneeling, dressed in a sumptuous golden cope studded with jewels. In this painting the master reached the highest point of his art, for he succeeded in putting into the face of the Pontiff all of his strong and authoritarian character, his lucid intelligence, his pride, his wilfulness and his overpowering sensuality. The remainder of the painting shows the hand of the pupils of the master, above all in the figure of Christ who is shown in a lozenge-shaped frame studded with golden beads. In the forefront on the right are three young soldiers who are certainly three contemporary portraits, perhaps Giovanni, Duke of Gandia, Cesare Borgia, and Jaffré, the sons of the Pope.

The Ascension in the lunette over the window should probably be attributed to Tiberio d'Assisi, while a rather higher artistic standard is achieved in the Pentecost, shown not, as usual, in the Room of the Last Supper, but in the open air.

The last of the mysteries is that of the Assumption of the Virgin, portrayed in a very graceful and simple manner.

The vault of the room is decorated with stuccos and pictures with figures of prophets, each of them holding in his hand a scroll with a Biblical passage relating to the Mystery portrayed below. The last room is the SALA dei PONTIFICI, so-called because it was especially adapted for official papal ceremonies. Originally it was roofed with a beam-ceiling, which collapsed in 1500, endangering the life of Alexander VI. The false vault which is now in the room was decorated with stuccos by Giovanni da Udine, and with grotesques by Perin del Vaga during the reign of Leo X (1513-1521).

Borgia Apartment - Room of the Saints - The Martyrdom of St. Sebastian, by Pinturicchio. In the background the Colosseum can be seen, while the church on the hill at the right may be that of Sts. John and Paul

Collection of Modern Religious Art - Bernard Buffet - Veronica

THE COLLECTION OF MODERN RELIGIOUS ART.

Founded on 23rd June 1973 by Paul VI, this collection is displayed in more than fifty rooms spread over two floors, beginning from the Borgia Apartment. It houses in all about eight hundred works by contemporary painters and sculptors, many of them still living. All the works are devoted to religious subjects.

Among the painters represented are Armando Spadini, Mario Sironi, Primo Conti, Francisco Goya, Henri Matisse, Ardengo Soffici, Corrado Cagli, Felice Carena, Bruno Cassinari, Domenico Purificato, Ferruccio Ferrazzi, Aldo Carpi, Pietro Annigoni, Virgilio Guidi, Gisberto Ceraccini, Carlo Carrà, Aligi Sasso, Emilio Greco, Maurice Denis, Silvio Consadori, Luigi Filocamo, Georges Roualt, Salvator Dali, Marc Chagall, Maurice Utrillo, Auguste Chabot, Giorgio Morandi, Filippo De Pisis, Massimo Campigli, Felice Casorati, Remo Wolf, Umberto Boccioni, Fiorenzo Tomea, Sante Monachesi, Giorgio de Chirico, Ottone Rosai, Bernard Ruffet, Ben Shahn, Abraham Ratzner, Gino Severini, Mirco, Towed Nicholas, Leon Lehmann, Gunter Hanzing.

There are also many sculptors, among them: Lello Scorzelli, Auguste Rodin, Romano Rui, Egidio Gerolli, Luciano Minguzzi, Francesco Nagni, Alessandro Monteleone, Francesco Messina, Pericle Fazzini, Mario Rudelli, Emilio o Greco, Aldo Carpi, Lucio Fontana, Narciso Cassino, Giacomo Manzù, Marino Marini, Publio Morbiducci, Venanzo Crocetti, Arturo Martini, Angelo Biancini, Floriano Bodini, Umberto Mastroianni, Leonard Baschin, Sahl Schwartz, Primo Conti, Amerigo Tot, Venanzio Blanco.

Sistine Chapel - Perugino - The donation of the Keys

THE SISTINE CHAPEL

The Sistine Chapel was built on the orders of Sixtus IV between 1475 and 1483 by Giovannino de'Dolci, on the basis of a design by Braccio Pontelli. It was meant to serve as a Chapel for the Palace, but at the same time it was also meant to act as a sort of small fortress, as can be seen from the battlemented upper part. It is made up of a rectangular (40.5 metres by 13.20) hall, 20 metres high, with a lowered barrel-vaulted ceiling which receives light from 12 large windows, six on each of the longer sides.

The flooring, which dates from the fifteenth century, is in the cosmatesque style. Mino da Fiesole, possibly with the aid of Andrea Bregno and Giovanni Dalmata, designed the beautiful marble transenna which divides the chapel into two unequal parts and also the balustrade of the choir.

In the Sistine Chapel the most important ceremonies have always been held, and still are today, in the presence of the Pope. Furthermore, it is here that the Conclave takes place (i.e. the meeting of the Cardinals after the death of each Pontiff, in order to elect his successor).

The frescos on the walls were painted between 1481 and 1483, following an iconographic pattern which was common at this time; above a lower section decorated with painted artificial curtains, there were (on the left) episodes from the life of Moses and (on the right) scenes from the life of Christ; in this way the history of mankind was summed up in two eras, one before the coming of the Messiah and one after it. For these frescos, Sixtus IV used the services of some of the greatest artists of the Renaissance: Perugino, Pinturicchio, Sandro Botticelli, Luca Signorelli, Cosimo Rosselli and Domenico Ghirlandaio.

Since the frescos of the far wall were destroyed to make way for Michelangelo's Last Judgment, and since some of the original frescos on the entrance wall have also been lost, having been refashioned in the sixteenth century, the Moses cycle now begins at the near end of the long side with *The Voyage of Moses into Egypt* by Perugino (1450-1510), which is followed by *The Youth of Moses* , one of the finest works of Sandro Botticelli, (1445-1510) suffused with a gentle atmosphere of dreamlike poetry in which the two legendary figures of the daughters of Jethro are also shown. In the third fresco, *The Crossing of the Red Sea* by Cosimo Rosselli (1439-1507) it is possible to make out the portrait of Cardinal Bessarion (the aged figure with the long beard and the red veil on his head , on the edge of the shore), and also likenesses of Virginio Orsini and Roberto Malatesta. Also by Rosselli is the *Giving of the Ten Commandments*. In the next fresco, Sandro Botticelli depicts scenes which are alive with pathos: The Punishment of Corah, Dathan and Abiram; in the background can be seen the Arch of Constantine and the ruins of the Septizonium, which in the fifteenth century was still decorated with columns. The cycle ends with the *Testament and Death of Moses* by Luca Signorelli (1441-1523) a youthful work of this artist, but one which was even so full of strength and power.

The events in the life of Christ begin — also at the end of the Chapel — with *The Baptism of Jesus* by the Umbrian School, and probably by Perugino and Pinturicchio.They continue with the *Purification of the Leper and the Temptations of Christ* by Sandro Botticelli (in the background the Roman Hospital of Santo Spirito symbolises the Temple of Jerusalem); *The Calling of Peter and Andrew*, by Domenico Ghirlandaio (1449-1494); *The Sermon on the Mount* and *The Healing of the Leper*, by Cosimo Rosselli, aided by Piero di Cosimo; *The Donation of the Keys*, by Perugino (assisted by Signroelli), and *The Last Supper*, by Cosimo Rosselli. *The Donation of the Keys* is Perugino's masterpiece: the principal scene and the minor scenes take place in the harmonious environment of a huge piazza, at the centre of which is the Temple of Jerusalem, in the form of a most elegant Renaissance building, flanked on either side by two arches of the type represented by Constantine's.

Sixtus IV also had the images of the first 31 Popes painted in the spaces between the windows. The figures of the first three pontiffs, and that of Jesus Himself, which were on the far wall, were sacrificed to leave space for the Last Judgment. There is some dispute among scholars as to who actually painted the individual portraits; most probably they were the work of Domenico Ghirlandaio, Cosimo Rosselli, Sandro Botticelli and Fra Diamante (1430- post 1498).

The vault of the Chapel was painted, according to the custom of the time, with an imitation of the blue sky studded with golden stars.

Sistine Chapel - Cosimo Rosselli - The Last Supper

Sistine Chapel ▶

The vault

When Giuliano della Rovere, Pope Julius II (1503-513) conceived the idea of having the ceiling of the Sistine Chapel repainted with portraits of the Twelve Apostles, despite the fact that he had at his disposal some of the most famous painters, all of them more or less experts in fresco-painting, a happy intuition led him to choose Michelangelo for the work. The artist himself would have preferred to devote himself to sculpture, but despite his own wishes he was forced to bow to the will of the Pope and on 10th May 1508 he began to paint the Apostles in the lunettes, according to the original scheme. However, Michelangelo's genius could not be held back in such severe limits, and since this work seemed to him "so poor", he obtained permission from the Pope to execute his own much more complex project, in the execution of which he worked unceasingly until the end of October 1512, often in conditions of extreme discomfort, sometimes painting lying flat on his back with the paint dripping on to his face for hours on end. He refused all the helpers whom contemporary artists normally made use of.

The result of this superhuman effort, however, was one of the greatest masterpieces of all time, and when the work was inaugurated, on 31st October 1512, it "was such as to make all the people amazed and dumbstruck" (Vasari). Michelangelo had managed to remain a sculptor even as he painted, giving his figures a superb quality of plastic motion, and fitting them into a vigorous architectonic framework. At the centre of the vault he had shown the primaeval events in the history of the world and of the human race, from the Creation and the First Sin to the Flood, thus linking them ideally to the story told on the walls, in that it is precisely because of sin that the redemptive coming of Christ was necessitated, while Noah is the figure who stands here as Moses' predecessor.

The first episode in the Creation cycle is that of the *Separation of Light and Darkness*; the second brings together the *Creation of the Sun, the Moon and the planets*. The third scene, with the *Separation of the*

Michelangelo - The Vault of the Sistine Chapel

Vault of the Sistine Chapel - the Separation of the Earth from the Waters, by Michelangelo

Vault of the Sistine Chapel - The Creation of Adam, by Michelangelo

Vault of the Sistine Chapel. Original Sin and the Expulsion from the Earthly Paradise, by Michelangelo ▶

IONAS

The sistine Chapel - The Cumaean Syvil (Michelangelo)

The Sistine Chapel: The Prophet Jonas, by Michelangelo

Waters from the Earth, is followed by one of the most fascinating scenes in the whole work *The Creation of Man*. Life is being transmitted from the Creator to the perfectly beautiful and harmonious figure of Adam only by means of the approach of their fingers. In *The Creation of Woman*, the very simple composition uses an intimate motion which gives it a sublime quality. The following scene, *The Original Sin*, is divided into two parts: the Temptation, and the Expulsion from the Garden. At the centre, the tree with the serpent represents the actual moment of the sin, the link between the two happenings. Here, as in the other scenes, the adherence to the Biblical narrative is perfect and very close: Eve, the protagonist, offers herself languidly to receive the apple of temptation, and shows her beautiful body without either provocation or shame.

In the episode of the Expulsion, on the other hand, an angel seen in foreshortened representation of a masterly kind is expelling the two actors in the drama, now rendered ugly by sin and with their faces transformed by sorrow, into a desert land, without hope. After *The Sacrifice of Moses* (interpreted by some, perhaps more accurately, as the Sacrifice of Cain and Abel), we come to the great depiction of the Universal Flood, which was the first to be painted by Michelangelo, and in which careful examination has revealed traces of rethinking and changes of style — perfectly comprehensible when we remember that a sculptor had been forced into the role of fresco-painter. Despite this the composition of the whole is full of strength, thanks to his powerful nudes, and to the study of various reactions of condemned humanity in the moment in which the fury of the elements was at its strongest. The cycle concludes with *The Drunkenness of Noah*, as a reminder that after the Flood the evils and the sins of the world were by no means at an end.

The nine scenes in the vault are of two different dimensions, and the minor illustrations alternate with the major ones — according to Condivi, Michelangelo's biographer and his contemporary; "so as to escape from the sense of satiety which results from too much similarity." At the corners of each of the minor scenes appear four powerful figures of naked young men, who in their incredible perfection of form marvelously embody their state of mind as they contemplate the scenes on the vault. On the corbels of the lunettes are painted seven prophets and five Sibyls, symbols of the conveying of the news of the Messiah's coming to the Jews and the Gentiles respectively.

The majestic prophetic figures are seated on marble thrones, and on the lateral pilasters of each of these there are a pair of cherubs functioning as caryatids. On the pilasters at the four corners of the vault are scenes which demonstrate the benevolence of God to his people, and the promise of redemption: *David and Goliath, Judith and Holofernes, The Prayer of Haman* and *The Bronze Serpent*. On the triangular veils adorning the lunettes above the windows can be seen the Ancestors of Christ, known from the Gospel of Matthew, while pairs of bronze nudes, with a mainly decorative function, are placed in the triangles of the veils, the vertices of which are linked to the cornice above by means of bucranes.

◀ *The Sistine Chapel - The Eritrean Sybil (Michelangelo)*

The Sistine Chapel - The Prophet Zachariah (Michelangelo)

Sistine Chapel - Michelangelo: The Delphic Sybil

Sistine Chapel - Michelange

ophet Jeremiah

Sistine Chapel - Michelangelo: The Prophet Ezekiel

IONAS

The Last Judgment

In 1533 Clement VII commissioned Michelangelo to complete the frescos of the Sistine Chapel with a *Fall of the Angels* on the entrance walls and a *Last Judgment* on the rear one. However the artist, even though he had accepted the commission, constantly tried to put off the work — partly because the sculptures for the tomb of Julius II were still occupying all his time. Finally it was the strong personality of Paul III (Farnese) which prevailed on him to take up his brushes again, and twenty-three years after the completion of the vault, Michelangelo began, in April 1535, to prepare the far wall of the Chapel for the great scene of the Last Judgment. It was necessary to wall up two windows and destroy the frescos by Perugino, as well as two lunettes with the ancestors of Christ by Michelangelo himself. The whole wall was lined with bricks, with a slight slope towards the base, to prevent the dust from settling there. Michelangelo worked alone at the great task for about five years, from the summer of 1536 to the autumn of 1541; achieving an incomparable masterpiece, and thanks to the great breadth of his own mind, going beyond every rule and every achievement so far attained in the history of art.

There is a whirling effect permeating the whole scene of the Day of the Wrath of God — the Dies Irae. The centre and dynamo of the whole picture is the terrible figure of Christ, as beautiful as a pagan deity, with a head inspired by that of the Apollo Belvedere and the body of a Hercules. He raises his arm in the implacable

Sistine Chapel - The Last Judgment, by Michelangelo (1536-1571)

Detail of the Last Judgement by Michelangelo: angels with the instruments of the Passion.

gesture of supreme justice, which at once rejects the evildoers and beckons to the righteous. Even the Elect are stricken with fear at this gesture, and the saints draw back with terror in their eyes. Beside Jesus, included in the halo of light surrounding him, is the Virgin Mother, and beside them stand the saints and martyrs displaying the instruments of their martyrdom — St Lawrence with his grill, St Catherine with the wheel, St Simeon with the saw, St Sebastian with the arrows, St Andrew and the Good Robber, Disma, with the Cross, and St Bartholemew holding his own skin, to which Michelangelo added a tragic self-portrait in the face. St John Baptist can be recognised by his clothing of animal-skins, while St Peter, defying all laws of perspective, is portrayed as larger even that the saints who stand in front of him because of his greater importance. Above Christ are the angels who are carrying the instruments of the divine passion, as justification for the implacability of the Judgment.

At the sound of the Last Trumpet of the Apocalypse, blown by angels who are in all respects akin to the pagan demons of the winds, the skeletons (lower left section) under the stupefied gaze of Death whose final defeat is signalled once and for all, rise up again from the earth and are reclothed in their flesh, in order to appear before Christ and be judged: from here the damned — some of them grasped by hideous devils, are hurled into the place where Charon loads them into his boat for the crossing to the Inferno, their eternal abode of sorrow.

The Sistine Chapel - Detail of the Last Judgement by Michelangelo, showing Christ the Judge and the Blessed Virgin

Detail of the Last Judgement by Michelangelo: Charon's boat

THE VATICAN PINACOTECA OR ART GALLERY

The idea of bringing together all the masterpieces of art belonging to the Papal States originated with a recommendation of the Congress of Vienna that the finest of the works which France restored to the Vatican should be put on public display; these works had been carried off by Napoleon's France as a result of the Treaty of Tolentino. The paintings were collected together by Pius VII in the Borgia Apartment in 1816. The collection was then moved around to various different sites, and it grew a great deal larger during Pius X's reign when the pictures from the Lateran and the Italian Primitives from the Biblioteca Apostolica were added to it. The present building was put up on the orders of Pius XI; designed by Luca Beltrami, it was opened in 1932. On that occasion the Gallery received a number of new works, and also the Arrasses from the Scuola

Vatican Gallery - Giotto: The Stefaneschi Triptych (c. 1300)

Vatican Gallery - Beato Angelico: (1400-1455): Madonna and Child between Saints Dominic and Catherine of Alexandria. ▶

TEMPLA DOMVM EXPOSITIS: VICOS FORA MOENIA PONTES:
VIRGINEAM TRIVII QVOD REPARARIS AQVAM.
PRISCA LICET NAVTIS STATVAS DARE COMMODA PORTVS:
ET VATICANVM CINGERE SIXTE IVGVM:
PLVS TAMEN VRBS DEBET: NAM QVAE SQVALORE LATEBAT:

Vatican Gallery - Melozzo da Forlì (1438-94): fresco showing Sixtus IV conferring the direction of the Apostolic Library on Platina

Vatican Gallery - The Crowning of the Virgin, by Pinturicchio (1450-1528)

Vecchia, woven on the basis of designs by Raphael.

The 1st ROOM contains exclusively Italian Primitives; there are numerous paintings on wood, most of them Byzantine, or of Byzantine inspiration; among them is a *Christ in Blessing* of the thirteenth century. There is a large altar-piece with the *Last Judgment* (end of the 11th or beginning of the 12th century), by the Benedictine School. Signed by two Roman painters, Niccolò and Giovanni, the work is in a very good state of preservation and shows many signs of classical influence. Beside this is a sharp and vigorous portrait of *St Francis of Assisi,* made by Margaritone d'Arezzo, a contemporary of the Saint (13th century). *The Funeral of St Francis* by Iacopo da Bologna, and the *Stories of the Life of St Francis,* by the School of Giunta Pisano, are also found here.

There are two works by Giovanni del Biondo, a Florentine painter of the fourteenth century; two wings of a triptych showing *Adoring Saints* and a *Madonna and Child with Saints.*

In the centre of the SECOND ROOM is the *Stefaneschi Polyptych,* which Giotto and his school painted in Rome, around 1300, for the altar of the *Confessio* of the ancient basilica on commission from Cardinal Stefaneschi. It is made up of three panels and a predella, painted on both sides. On the main side the central panel has *Christ enthroned, surrounded by angels;* on the left panel is the *Crucifixion of St Peter* and on the right the *Martyrdom of St Paul,* while on the predella there is a painting of the *Madonna and Child and Twelve Apostles.* On the other side the central panel has *St Peter enthroned* with Cardinal Stefaneschi kneeling at his feet and holding this very triptych in his hand. On the side panels are *St James, St Paul, St Mark and St John.*

There are also many works by Italian painters of the fourteenth century, some belonging to the Florentine school like Bernadino Daddi (*The Madonna of the Magnificat*) and Lorenzo Monaco (*The Miracles of St Benedict* and *The Crib*), or to the Sienese School, like Simone Martini (c.1285-1344), the painter of the *Redeemer in Blessing,* and Ambrogio Lorenzetti, to whom the *Stories of St Stephen* has been attributed.

A lovely *Annunciation* by Giovanni di Paolo was originally the cover of an account book of the City Government of Siena, dated 1444.

The most famous works in ROOM III are those of Fra' Giovanni da Fiesole, known as Beato Angelico (1400-1455) the painter who had the hidden art of infusing all his works with a profound spirituality. The tableau with *The Virgin Between Saints Dominic and Catherine of Egypt* shows a great delicacy and finesse, while the *Stories of St Nicholas of Bari* has great vigour and a deep sense of colour. These were part of the predella of a polyptych in the Church of St Dominic in Perugia; in the Art Gallery of that city the polyptych itself and one of the scenes from the predella are still preserved.

Among the other fifteenth century masterpieces in this room are a *Coronation of the Virgin* by Filippo Lippi (1406 to 1469) and the *Madonna of the Girdle* by Benozzo Gozzoli (1420-97).

The 4th ROOM is exclusively given up to works by Melozzo da Forlì (1438-94) and his pupil Marco Palmezzano (1456-1543). The famous fresco representing *Platina receiving the office of Prefect of the Apostolic Library from Sixtus IV* is by Melozzo; in this work the portraits achieve a remarkable synthesis between portraiture and idealisation of the type. In this Room there are also numerous fragments of the large fresco by Melozzo which decorated the apse of the Basilica of the Twelve Apostles in Rome, which were taken down from the walls before the choir of the church was totally demolished for restoration. The paintings by Marco Palmezzano include a *Madonna with Child and Saints,* and a *Madonna and Child enthroned, surrounded by Sts John the Baptist and Jerome, and an angel playing a musical instrument.*

On the right-hand wall is a huge *Flemish arras,* given in October 1533 by Francis I to Clement VII. It is the most ancient existing copy of *The Last Supper* by Leonardo.

In the 5th ROOM there are some fifteenth century paintings, among them a predella with the *Miracles of St Vincenzo Ferreri* by the Ferrarese painter Francesco Cossa (1435-1477), a *Holy Family* by Palmezzano, and a *Pietà* by the German Lucas Cranach (1472-1553).

Polyptychs and altarpieces are collected in the 6th ROOM; among the most interesting are a *Madonna and Child* and a *Pietà* by Carlo Crivelli (1430-1495), a Venetian painter with an incisive and sober use of colour. The polyptych of the *Madonna and Child with Saints,* dated 1481, is by his brother and pupil Vittore Crivelli.

The *Crucifixion* and the *Polyptych of Montelpare* by Niccolò da Foligno, known as l'Alunno (c1430-1502) is marked by a strong — and sometimes exaggerated — expressive feeling. There is a polyptych by Antonio Vivarini, with *St Anthony the Abbot, eight Saints* and *Christ coming forth from the Sepulchre;* it is dated 1469, and still shows a good deal of Gothic influence..

The 7th ROOM is given over to the artists of the Umbrian School of the fifteenth century, who were fond of a clean and 'calligraphic' line, and very bright colours. There is a great *Coronation of the Virgin* by Pinturicchio (1454-1513), and a fragment of a fresco showing a *Madonna and Child.* Another *Madonna and Saints* and *an Adoration of the Magi* are the work of Spagna (1450-1528).

Among the principal works by Perugino (1445-1523)

Vatican Gallery - Perugino: Madonna in Glory ▶

HOC ·PETRVS·DECHASTRO PLEBIS·PINXIT

◀ *Vatican Gallery -*
Raphael: Madonna of Foligno (1512-13)

Vatican Gallery -
The Transfiguration, Raphael's last work

is the *Madonna Enthroned* shown here; a painting which shows a lively but balanced use of colour. In this room one can also see what remains of Perugino's predella, with *St Benedict, St Flavia and St Placidus*. The *St Jerome* signed by Giovanni Santi of Urbino, Raphael's father, is a rather mediocre work, but the *Madonna and Child with St John* is a delicate work full of poetry; it is by an unknown Umbrian artist.

The 8th ROOM is entirely dedicated to Raphael (1483-1520). In the *Coronation of Mary*, painted by the great master when we was only twenty years old, in 1503, we can feel very strongly Perugino's influence; he was Raphael's master — but the artist's greatness and originality can already be sensed, in embryo at least, in the search for naturalism and the rejection of convention. On the predella of this panel are painted an *Annunciation*, an *Epiphany* and a *Presentation of Jesus in the Temple*.

At the centre of the far wall is the *Madonna of Foligno*, painted by Raphael on a panel between 1512 and 1513, but transferred to canvas in the nineteenth century. The work was destined for the Church of Santa Maria in Aracoeli; it was commissioned by Sigismond de' Conti, the Secret Chamberlain of Julius II, as a thank-offering for having miraculously escaped death when a bomb blew up his house during a siege at Foligno.

From this painting the full maturity of the great artist can be clearly seen; it is shown in the purity of line, the naturalness and harmony of every individual gesture, the rich but at the same time controlled chromatic effects. The Virgin, with her beautiful face suffused with gentleness, is seated on the clouds, surrounded by a halo of light, and with her Divine Son in her arms; he seems to want to get down and play with a delightful little angel who is looking up and holding in his hand a shield on which the miracle of the bomb must once have been described; it is depicted in the background. On the left of the painting are *St John Baptist and St Francis*, while to the right *St Jerome* is presenting the donor of this work, Sigismondo de' Conti, to the Virgin.

The *Transfiguration* belongs to the last and most complex period of Raphael's art, in which the master suceeded in uniting Florentine purity of design, invigorated by Michelangelo's anatomical studies, with Venetian strength of coloration.

Unfortunately, Raphael died (at the age of 36, on Good Friday, 6th April 1520) before he finished the upper part of the work. The painting was placed at the head of his funeral couch: "which work, when they saw the living and the dead bodies together, made the hearts of all those present break with sorrow" (Vasari).

The Transfiguration' was completed by Giulio Romano and Giovan Francesco Penni, and was placed in the Church of San Pietro in Montorio, where it remained until 1797.

The work has recently been restored, and can now be seen in all its beauty. It shows Christ flanked by Moses and Elijah, and surrounded by a brilliant halo of light which seems to be drawing him towards the sky. At the summit of Mount Tabor, Peter, James and John appear to be flooded with divine light and at the same time terrified by it, while at the left we can see St Laurence and St Julian kneeling. In the lower part of the painting the other apostles are shown, together with numerous people who are surrounding a child possessed by a demon.

In the same room there are also the *ten arrases* of the *Scuola Vecchia*, for which Raphael made the cartoons in 1516 (now in the Victoria and Albert Museum in London) which were woven in Brussels by Pieter Van Aelst. The subjects of these arrases are: *the Blinding of Elymas* (the lower half of this is missing, destroyed during the Sack of Rome in 1527); *the Conversion of St Paul;* the *Stoning of St Stephen; St Peter healing a cripple*, the *Death of Ananias;* the *Bestowing of the Keys;* the *Miraculous Draught of Fishes; Saint Paul Preaching in Athens*, the *Sacrifice of Lystra* and *St. Paul in prison*.

In the 9th ROOM there are paintings from the fifteenth and sixteenth centuries, among them the famous *St Jerome* of Leonardo da Vinci, which although it is unfinished, shows all the greatness of this many-sided genius. The painting, which was owned in the eighteenth century by the woman painter Angelica Kauffmann, was subsequently lost; in the first years of the nineteenth century Cardinal Fasch, Napoleon's uncle, found it in the store-room of a Roman antique dealer, but without the head; the lucky prelate eventually succeeded in finding this, too, in a cobbler's workshop.

Among the other works in this little room, one of the most outstanding is a *Pietà* by Giovanni Bellini (c1430-1516); this was the upper part of a polyptych in the Church of St Francis at Pesaro, now in the Art Gallery of that town.

The 10th ROOM contains works from the sixteenth century Venetian school, whose greatest representative was Titian (Tiziano Vecellio) (1477-1576). His amazing altarpiece of the *Madonna and Child* and *Sts Sebastian, Francis, Anthony of Padua, Peter, Nicholas and Cat-*

Vatican Art Gallery - Leonardo da Vinci (1452-1519) St. Jerome. ▶

herine is displayed here; he painted it in 1528 for the Church of the Frati in Venice. The upper part of the work is missing — the scallop in which the Holy Spirit was portrayed in the form of a dove amid rays of light. But we can still appreciate the fulness of Titian's art in its maturity, made up essentially of light and colour.

Paolo Caliari, known as Veronese, (1528-1588) was the painter of the *St Helena,* which is rich and vibrant with light. In the same room there is large altar-piece, known as the *Madonna of Monteluce,* painted by Giulio Romano (1490-1528) on the basis of a drawing by Raphael, after the master's death. *The Saint George killing the Dragon* by Paris Bordone (1500-1571) is also worth noting.

In the 11th ROOM there are works by painters of the late sixteenth century, among them Barocci (1528-1612), represented here by an *Annunciation,* the delightful *Madonna with the cherries,* and a realistic portrait of *Beata Michaelina.*

Giorgio Vasari, author of 'The Lives of the Most Excellent Painters, Sculptors and Architects' is represented here by a mediocre *Stoning of St Stephen,* full of rhetorical gesture, while Giuseppe Cesari, known as the Cavalier d'Arpino (1568-1640) is the author of the cold *Annunciation,* painted in 1606. In this room there are also works by Girolamo Muziano (1528-1590), among them a canvas with the *Raising of Lazarus* which won praise from Michelangelo. A fresh and somewhat naif *Assumption* carries the signature of Nicola Filotesio, known as Cola dell'Amatrice (1489-1559).

The 13th ROOM, which is octagonal, has some of the most famous works in the whole Pinacoteca, beginning with the Deposition, painted between 1602 and 1604 by Michelangelo Merisi, known as Caravaggio (1573-1601). The figures emerge from the very obscure background thanks to a violent light which increases the dramatic character of the scene. The realism of the work is increased by the fact that each of the persons in it faithfully represents a type studied by the artist in the streets, among the common people, as was his custom.

To the right of the entrance door is the *Crucifixion of St Peter* by Guido Reni (1575-1642); there is also another picture by Reni here — the *Virgin in Glory with Saints Thomas and Jerome.*

Among the most famous works in this room is the *Communion of St Jerome,* by Domenico Zamieri, known as Domenichino (1581-1641). Three paintings by Guercino (1591-1666) also deserve mention: *St Thomas, St Catherine of Cortona* and a *Magdalen with Angels.* There is also the *Martyrdom of St Erasmus* by Poussin, the most important French painter of the seventeenth century.

In the 13th ROOM are pictures from the seventeenth and eighteenth centuries. A large canvas showing *St Francesco Saverio* is attributed, with some likelihood, to Antonio Van Dyck (1559-1641). The *Judith of* Orazio Gentileschi is a striking and original work; equally interesting are two paintings by Pietro da Cortona (1596-1669): the *Virgin appearing to St Francis* and *a Satyr conquered by Cupid.* The *Martyrdom of St Laurence,* which clearly shows the influence of Caravaggio, is attributed to Jusepe Ribera, known as Lo Spagnoletto (1588-1656) or to his pupil E. Somer (1615-1684).

Various works by Italian and foreign painters of the seventeenth and eighteenth centuries are to be found in the 14th ROOM — the most noteworthy are the *Triumph of Death* by Pieter Paul Rubens (1577-1640), and two works by Nicholas Poussin, (*the Victory of Gideon over the Midianites* and *Saint Erasmus.*)

The 15th ROOM has many portraits, including those of the *Doge Niccolò Marcello* by Titian, *George IV of England* by Thomas Lawrence (1769-1830), *Pius VI* by Pompeo Batoni (1708-87) *Benedict XIV* by Giuseppe Maria Crespi, (1665-1747) *Cardinal Girolamo Albani* by Sassoferrato (1609-85) and *Clement IX* by Carlo Maratta (1625-1713).

. In the 15th and last ROOM are a few modern paintings, including a St Mark in Venice by Ippolito Caffi (1809-1866).

Vatican Gallery - Domenico Zampieri, known as Dominichino: The Communion of St. Jerome ▶

◀ *Vatican Gallery - Federico Fiori, know as Barocci (1528-1612) Rest during the Flight into Egypt (The Madonna of the Cherries)*

Vatican Gallery - Michelangelo Merisi, known as Caravaggio - The Deposition (1604) ▶

THE MUSEO GREGORIANO PROFANO

The Museum was instituted by Gregory XVI in 1844; originally it was located in the ground floor of the Lateran Palace. During the pontificate of Pius IX it was greatly enriched by material from the excavations at Ostia (1857), and in the last years of the nineteenth century and the first years of our own, a great collection of epigraphical works was added.

During the pontificate of John XXIII, the Museum was trasferred from the Lateran to the Vatican, in a building erected for it by the Passarelli brothers.

The first Section contains Roman copies or reworkings of original Greek models. Of special interest are: a statue of Marsyas and a torso of the same figure, and a head of Pallas Athene — copies of the famous group of Athene and Marsyas by Myron (fifth century B.C.) which was once on the Acropolis in Athens. One of the most outstanding portraits is that of Sophocles, a copy of the work of Cephisodotus and Tymarcos, the sons of Praxiteles, which stood in the Theatre of Dionysus in Athens. There is a huge statue of Neptune placing his foot on the prow of a ship — a replica of a fourth century B.C. original. Also of some interest is the Hellenistic relief (1st century B.C.) showing a woman with a comic poet, holding the mask of comedy in his hand. This is possibly a Muse and Menander, the greatest representative of the 'New Comedy' in Greece in the fourth century B.C.

The Second Section is devoted to Roman sculpture of the first century and the early part of the second; it has numerous portrait-figures, sume funerary reliefs and bas-relief of the Claudian era, in which there are three personifications of Etruscan cities - Vetulonia, Vulci and Tarquinia, possibly part of the throne made for the great statue of Claudius wearing the crown of oak, which is displayed in the same room. There is a similar statue of Tiberius, portrayed in the likeness of Jove. and two reliefs, one of them with a sacrificial procession, coming from the Altar known as the Vicomagistri, while the other one shows a procession of magistrates in front of a temple. The upper part of this relief is only a cast of the original fragment, which is in the National Roman Museum. The busts of a man and a woman of the **gens Ateria** in small niches are some of the best existing examples of Roman portraiture of the first century A.C.

The Third Section contains the sarcophagi, some of them decorated with interesting reliefs, like the three which come from a tomb near the Porta Viminalis, showing the myth of Orestes, with masks and bunches of fruit, and the destruction of the children of Niobe.

The Roman sculpture of the second and third centuries is displayed in the Fourth Section; it includes a fine torso from a loricated statue made from porphyry.

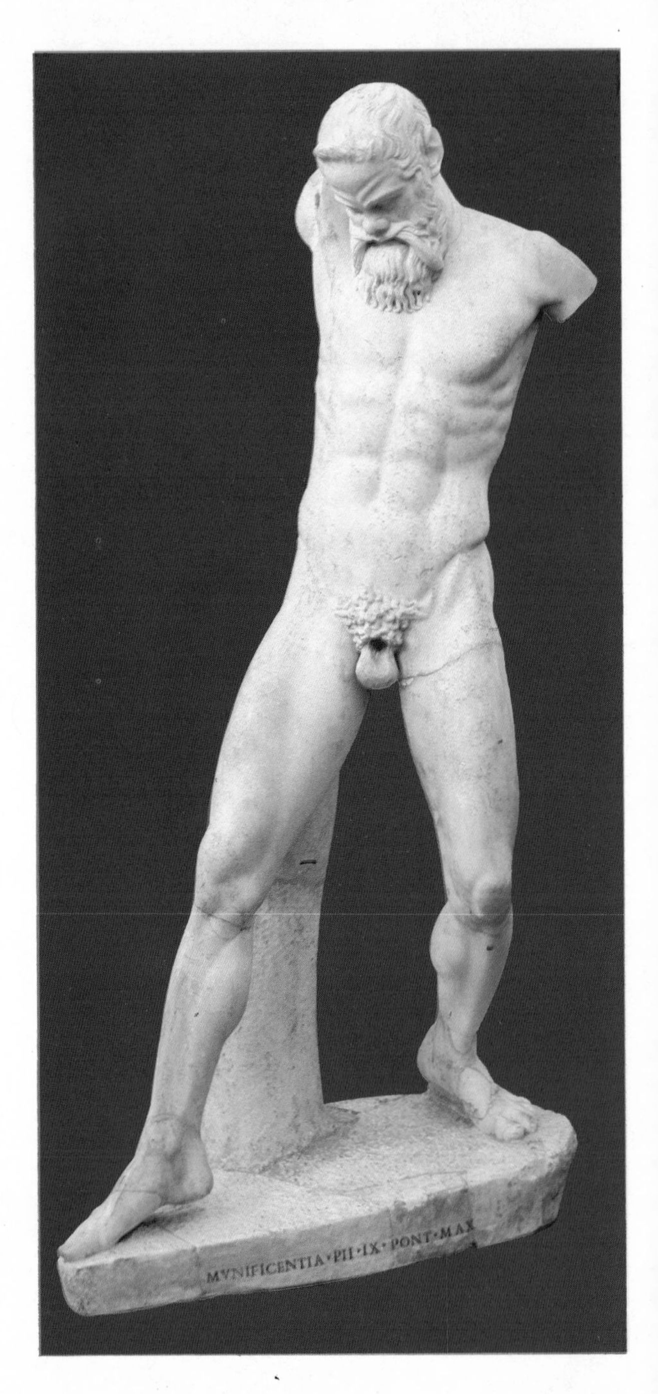

Museo Gregoriano Profano - Statue of Marsas from the Roman copy of the famous group of Athena and Marsyas by Myron 5th cent. BC)

THE PIO CRISTIANO MUSEUM

The Museum was founded by Pius IX, who instituted it in 1854 with the aim of collecting together all the material from the Catacombs which could not be housed on the spot. The collection, which until 1963 was kept in the Lateran Palace, is divided into two sections, the first made up of sculpture, mosaics and architectural exhibits, while the second, which is still in process of assembly, is made up of inscriptions.

Among the most important pieces in the Museum is the fragmentary inscription from the memorial stone to Abericius, a Phrygian bishop of the era of Marcus Aurelius (161 - 180 A.D.). It is the oldest Christian inscription with a Eucharistic content.

There are many sarcophagi, some of them decorated with interesting reliefs, such as the 3rd or 4th century one coming from San Lorenzo fuori le Mura, of which the front section has survived, showing Christ among the twelve Apostles and fifteen sheep, a symbol of the Church. On a sarcophagus from the Pretestato Cemetery on the Via Appia three shepherds are shown; the one in the centre is carrying a ram on his shoulder while the two on either side have sheep; around them there is a lively scene of a harvest (fourth century work). The sarcophagus known as the 'Dogmatic' was found during the work for the foundations of the baldacchino of Saint Paul's-without-the-Walls, and is decorated only on the front side, with scenes from the Old and New Testaments, in two ranks on either side of a clipeus showing bust portraits of the two people whose tomb this was (first half of the fourth century).

Towards the end of this Room are exhibited some fragments of sarcophagi showing the birth of Jesus and the Epiphany, among them a lid which shows the Wise Men offering gifts to the Child; Jesus in in swaddling clothes in a manger among the oxen and donkeys. There is also a scene of Daniel in the Lions' Den, a protrait of the owner of the tomb herself (whose name was Crispina), the Miracle of the loaves, the capture of St Peter, and the Miracle of the Spring. (mid fourth century).

The most famous sculpture in the Museum is the statue, unfortunately heavily restored, of the Good Shepherd, shown in the fashion of the iconography (already popular in the pagan world) of the Chriophorus, or the shepherd with the sheep on his shoulder. Here the shepherd is Christ himself, represented as a young man with no beard and long hair down to his shoulders, dressed in a short, sleeveless tunic and with a shoulder-bag.

The sheep which he is carrying represents the Church itself, defended and protected by its Shepherd.

Pio Cristiano Museum - The Good Shepherd (3rd - 4th century)

THE MISSIONARY AND ETHNOLOGICAL MUSEUM

This Museum also comes from the Lateran, where it was set up by Pius XI in 1926 with objects from the Vatican Missionary Exhibition of 1925, and with donations from private individuals and various institutions. Its aim is to illustrate the missionary activities of the Church in various parts of the world, at the same time demonstrating the usages and customs of the peoples of Asia, Oceania, Africa, America and Australasia.

Some of the carriages on display in the Historical Museum ▶

The Missionary and Ethnological Museum - Adoration of the Magi, by an unknown Indian artist

THE MUSEO STORICO

The Historical Museum was founded in 1973 and is housed in rooms below the so-called Giardino Quadrato.

It is made up of two sections, in which are displayed papal carriages, uniforms of the Papal armed Corps, steel weapons, culverins and bombards. Portraits of the Commanders of the Noble Guard adorn the walls of the Second Section.

The Vatican Gardens

THE VATICAN GARDENS

In the western part of Vatican City, between the walls and the Papal Palace, are the extremely beautiful gardens, with their greens and copses, crossed by pathways and ornamented by artifical caves, monumental fountains and pavilions, in the tradition of the Italian gardens of the sixteenth century.

Near the Ethiopian College is a concrete reproduction of the famous Grotto of Lourdes, which the French Catholics offered as a gift to Leo XIII; near this place there is an incomparable view over Rome and the surrounding countryside. When we pass beyond this point, the road runs alongside a well-preserved section of the wall erected by Nicholas V in the fifteenth century, on which stands the Tower of Saint John. A little way from here one can see the buildings of the original Vatican Radio Station.

To continue our visit to the Gardens, we should turn back towards the Grotto of Lourdes, and carry on alongside another stretch of the walls of Nicholas V until we reach the small turret which houses Vatican Radio; behind this is the little church of the Madonna della Guardia, built during the pontificate of Benedict XV. From here we come to one of the most picturesque of all the fountains in the garden, the one called the Fountain of the Rock (dello Scoglio) or of the Great Eagle (dell'Aquilone) by Johan Van Santen (1550-1621); it is made up of a large basin from which a great eagle in tufa is rising.

We then go on in the direction of the Papal Palaces, and we come to the Little House (Casina) of Pius IV, commissioned by Paul IV in 1558 from Pirro Ligorio. The Pope wanted to make a small villa where the Popes could go and rest during the spring and autumn. When Paul IV died, the building was completed by his successor Pius IV. Pirro Ligorio, aided by Sallustio, the son of Baldassarre Peruzzi, succeeded in creating a real masterpiece of architectural harmony.

The loggia has a fairly simple façade, facing east,

with the lower part surrounded by a 'fishpond', and decorated with three niches, a central one with an arch and two rectangular sides ones, where several statues are placed. In the upper part there is a characteristic loggetta, crowned by a Tympanum with the arms of Pius IV. The façade which looks towards the courtyard has no loggetta, and is elaborately decorated with stucco work depicting mythological subjects. The oval courtyard is surrounded by a low wall along which there runs a marble bench interrupted by the entrance to the villa and to the loggia, and by two ornamental niches with stucco and mosaic decoration. At the centre of the courtyard is a little fountain with two cupids sitting on dolphins. The actual villa has a façade covered with rich decoration, divided into three orders, while inside there are only two floors above the ground.The internal decoration is also luxurious, with mirror vaulting decorated by vey delicate plaster-work, and by paintings from artists such as Federico Zuccari, Santi di Tito and Barocci. As we go down towards the Sistine Chapel, which can be easily recognised from its crenellation, we arrive at the Palace of the Mint, at the side of which there is another fountain by Johan Van Santen — in this case known as 'The Sacrament' Fountain, with two crenellated towers from which the dragons of the arms of Paul V (Borghese) appear.

The Vatican Gardens

THE PONTIFICAL AUDIENCE CHAMBER

The Great Audience Chamber was inaugurated in 1971, and was designed by Pier Luigi Nervi, who conceived it in the shape of a shell, linking the huge precast concrete vault with the body of the auditorium by very original means. Because of its exceptional dimensions, the Chamber can house as many as 12,000 people. At the far end is the great relief of Christ of the Blessings, by Pericle Fazzini.

Interior of the Pontifical Audience Chamber

INDEX OF ILLUSTRATIONS

Printed in Italy by
Tipografia Arti Grafiche Libra - Roma
March 1983

L. 7000
(IVA inclusa)